T0170357

Clarence Major is the prize-winning author of four novels, five collections of poems, a critical study of Black American literature, a dictionary of Afro-American slang, and editor of an anthology. His works have been translated into German, Italian, French, Spanish and other languages and he has been the recipient of grants from the National Council on the Arts, the State Department, the New York Cultural Foundation and the Holland Festival in Rotterdam. Major's poetry won the 1976 Pushcart Prize and his shorter works appear in over a hundred anthologies and periodicals. Major teaches literature and creative writing and gives lectures and readings at universities and colleges around the country.

FICTION COLLECTIVE
Books in Print:

The Second Story Man by Mimi Albert
Althea by J. M. Alonso
Searching for Survivors by Russell Banks
Babble by Jonathan Baumbach
Chez Charlotte and Emily by Jonathan Baumbach
Reruns by Jonathan Baumbach
Things in Place by Jerry Bumpus
∅ *Null Set* by George Chambers
Amateur People by Andrée Connors
Take It or Leave It by Raymond Federman
Museum by B. H. Friedman
Temporary Sanity by Thomas Glynn
The Talking Room by Marianne Hauser
Holy Smoke by Fanny Howe
Mole's Pity by Harold Jaffe
Moving Parts by Steve Katz
Find Him! by Elaine Kraf
Emergency Exit by Clarence Major
Reflex and Bone Structure by Clarence Major
The Secret Table by Mark Mirsky
Encores for a Dilettante by Ursule Molinaro
Rope Dances by David Porush
The Broad Back of the Angel by Leon Rooke
The Comatose Kids by Seymour Simckes
Fat People by Carol Sturm Smith
The Hermetic Whore by Peter Spielberg
Twiddledum Twaddledum by Peter Spielberg
Long Talking Bad Conditions Blues by Ronald Sukenick
98.6 by Ronald Sukenick
Meningitis by Yuriy Tarnawsky
Statements 1
Statements 2

*Risking a Somersault
in the Air*

Risking a Somersault in the Air

Conversations with Nicaraguan Writers

by Margaret Randall

translated by Christina Mills

edited by Floyce Alexander

CURBSTONE PRESS

© 1984 Margaret Randall
All rights reserved

Originally published in 1984
by Solidarity Publications, San Francisco, CA
First release by Curbstone Press in 1990

cover design by Jane Norling

printed in the U.S. by McNaughton & Gunn

Photographs on pages 66, 88, 140, 170 and 219
are by Rick Reinhard; all other photographs are
by Margaret Randall

Library of Congress number 86-10052
ISBN: 0-915306-92-1

distributed in the U.S. by
InBOOK
140 Commerce St.
East Haven, CT 06512

published by
CURBSTONE PRESS
321 Jackson St., Willimantic, CT 06226

This book is for my brother
John Randall
and his bookshop in Albuquerque

Contents

Introduction   1

Sergio Ramírez   21

Vidaluz Menéses   41

Lizandro Chávez Alfaro   55

Carlos Guadamuz   67

Beltrán Morales   79

Ernesto Cardenal   89

Michele Najlis   109

Omar Cabezas   119

Gioconda Belli   141

Daisy Zamora   155

Francisco de Asís Fernández   171

Milagros Palma   185

Julio Valle-Castillo   193

Tomás Borge   205

Introduction

Philadelphia photographer Jack Levine gave me the idea for this book when we talked in Managua almost two years ago. He commented on the fact that so many men and women in high posts in Nicaragua's government are writers, many of them exceptional poets. And he contrasted that fact with the image of these leaders (and writers) projected by the U.S. establishment press.

We talked about what art means in a consumer society, and what it means in Nicaragua's new society, where people who have come through a costly war are building a world in which every value is picked up, held, examined, weighed against the obstacles that would ignore or crush it, and is then either rejected or nurtured.

In Latin America, of course, it would be unfair to claim that a deep appreciation of artistic expression was born with revolutionary change. It goes far back. Somehow—in spite of slavery, genocide, colonialism, neocolonialism, banana republic politics, dictators thought to be fictions when described as they actually are, relentless oppression and repression, new categories of human pain (such as the massive number of "disappeared" and the hundreds of thousands who have been exiled), military juntas, and freewheeling death squads—a people's culture has survived and grown on this continent.

I remember a customs official in Mexico once begging me for an autographed copy of a book of my poems, when I answered his perfunctory "What's your occupation?" with the word "poet." North American poet Floyce Alexander reminded me recently of a conversation with a Cuban diplomat in Mexico City in the sixties. The representative of the Cuban Revolution had asked Floyce if he'd ever thought of going to Cuba. "What could I do there?" was Floyce's reply, thinking, as he was, of the island's need for doctors and technicians. "Well, you're a poet, aren't you?" the man answered.

The idea that a poet is necessary to society, and the dignity and strength such necessity carries with it, is a concept as hard to come by in twentieth-century U.S. life as it is complex and difficult to explore, even in a country like Nicaragua. Or, perhaps, especially in a country like Nicaragua—today. The war that should have ended five years ago still rages along northern and southern borders. U.S.-backed Somoza men have taken several thousand lives (more than half of them civilian) in these years since the Sandinista victory. As important as poetry is considered to be in a country like Nicaragua, priorities in production and defense still necessarily demand the full-time attention of everyone—including poets. Still, the relationship between poetry and ordinary human activity is unique in Nicaragua. Poetry *is* an ordinary human activity there.

Attempting to understand the Nicaraguan's relationship to poetry—and to creativity in general—recalls Haydeé Santamaría's[1] description of her first meeting with Ho Chi Minh. "I didn't know if Ho was the way he was because he was Vietnamese," she said, "or if the Vietnamese people were the way

---

1. Haydeé Santamaría, Cuban heroine of the attack on Moncada Barracks (July 26th, 1953) and an important participant throughout the history of the Cuban Revolution, was since its founding and for many years the president of the Casa de las Américas, the prestigious Latin American cultural institution. She committed suicide in 1980.

they were because they had someone like Ho Chi Minh." In Nicaraguan history, the great modernist poet Rubén Darío is a strong figure, not just for literary people but for workers and farmers who possess a relatively low educational level. Attempting to trace the importance of poetry in the lives of Nicaraguans, one logically goes back to Darío. And to Alfonso Cortés, Solomón de la Selva, Joaquín Pasos, Manolo Cuadra, and Edwin Castro. The question is posed: Was Rubén Darío (or Cortés, de la Selva, Pasos, Cuadra, or Castro) the poet he was because, among other things, he came from that violent expanse of volcanic strength called Nicaragua? Or do Nicaraguans owe the particular way poetry is important in their lives to Darío?

Poetry, dance, street theater, and song are deep traditions among the Nicaraguans. Local religious festivals in Masaya, León, Diriamba, Granada, and elsewhere are rich in distinctive cultural expressions: dances, costumes, masks, collective games, ritual verses, and the very presentation of the saints themselves. "Sociodramas" (spontaneous theatrical sketches dealing with social problems) were used throughout the years of popular struggle and continue to be used in educational work today by people in the neighborhoods and mass organizations.

In the months following the 1979 victory, delegations from remote villages and towns would show up at the newly founded Ministry of Culture, demanding attention to their People's Culture Houses. Perhaps they had just taken over the home of a fleeing *somocista* (Somoza supporter) and their group impulse was to use it not as a clinic or school but as a gathering place for those who felt the need to sing, write, paint, dance; in short, to express themselves artistically. They brought long lists of their immediate needs: twenty guitars (with extra sets of strings), watercolors, ballet slippers, a kiln. Representatives from the ministry, on official visits to France or Bulgaria, began to ask for supplies for the primitive painters of Jinotega or for a darkroom for Boaco's beginning photographers.

It wasn't always easy. Or it was never easy. Major percentages of the national budget were going to health and education. Hospitals and schools constituted urgent needs. The literacy campaign, which for nearly half the country's population provided their first opportunity to read and write, took almost a year's intense activity. Meanwhile, every day dozens and then hundreds of street kids swarmed the elegant gardens of the Ministry of Culture, running across the tennis courts and swimming in the pool. Before July 1979 these grounds had been off-limits to anyone but the dictator's inner circle.

I evoke these things from memories of Managua—and of other parts of the country—in those months just following the people's victory. I want to define the specific place occupied by poets and poetry in Nicaraguan society, and how that place has changed with the advent of the revolution. And I know it's still pretty impressionistic. Here's another piece for the puzzle.

In the Spanish language, university graduates are referred to in conversations as *Licenciado* or *Licenciada: Licenciado Gómez . . . Licenciada Martínez . . .* A doctor is called Doctor just about anywhere. But Nicaragua is the only country I've known where a poet is referred to by that "title" preceding his or her name. That says something about the love and respect afforded versemakers in the country. Someone will call out, *"Poeta Cardenal . . . Poeta Belli . . ."* or simply "Hey, poet . . ." when trying to catch that person's attention.

The poem also had a fundamental role to play on the walls of this country during the long years of recent struggle, especially during the insurrectional period from 1977 to 1979. *Pintas* was what they called the messages, painted during the night with spray cans or with stencils, which appeared each morning in every city, town, and village. Some said simply: LONG LIVE THE FSLN; IN THE MOUNTAINS WE'LL BURY THE ENEMY'S HEART; GOD BLESS A MOTHER WHO GIVES BIRTH TO A SANDINIST CHILD; IF TOMAS DIES . . . (with suggestive ellipses, and referring to Tomás Borge, who was on a hunger strike that had reached its fifty-ninth day at the time this *pinta* appeared simultaneously throughout Nicaragua); GUARD, DESERT! GIVE YOUR WEAPON TO THE PEOPLE!

But in other *pintas* the clandestine painter risked a longer interval of activity and placed on the wall an entire poem that would speak to his sisters and brothers on the following morning. Poems by Rigoberto López Pérez (the young man who sacrificed his own life when he put an end to Somoza García's on September 21st, 1956), Edwin Castro, Leonel Rugama, and Ricardo Morales were especially popular. There were times when the combatant wrote his or her own poem. The originality of the *pintas* speaks of the ingenuity and creativity of Nicaraguans as a whole, and the profusion attests to their audacity. A complex organization was needed to successfully carry out this task of painting the walls; you needed to keep your paint in one house, your brushes and stencils in another (both near where you intended to work), and while one comrade painted others had to be standing guard for possible discovery by the enemy (I don't think it's necessary to emphasize the fact that discovery meant death). Yet, as I say, the country was one big compendium of *pintas* by July 19th, 1979. In a recent conversation, Commander Dora María Tellez linked the phenomena to the current discussion of press censorship in the country. "You can't censor the walls," she laughed. "If people today really felt they had something to say that they weren't being allowed to say in print or on the radio, every wall in this country would tell us about it!"

Since the victory, the tendency has been for people to want to repair and paint their homes. The destruction was heavy during the war; people yearn for a peacetime panorama (along with peace itself). Some of the most significant *pintas* have been preserved as one would salvage living history for a museum. But the same ingenuity, sense of humor, inventiveness, and talent now go into the creation of people's slogans shouted by thousands of voices at rallies and marches. Many of these slogans are extremely poetic. Politically or socially oriented billboards display the poetry that formerly was scrawled hurriedly on walls. Poems have become songs.

Throughout Nicaraguan culture, the poet is the high priest. The prophet. The maker of visions. The singer of songs. The one who knows and can say it for others the way others feel it but cannot say it for themselves. Throughout the conversations in this book, more than one writer interviewed remembers early childhood meetings with older poets, meetings conducted with the respect—reverence even—afforded those who make poems.

In early 1983 Rosario Murillo—herself a poet—suggested I do a series of interviews with Nicaraguan writers for *Ventana,* the weekly cultural supplement of the FSLN's daily newspaper, *Barricada.* I began speaking with the writers, photographing them, taking a new look at some of their work. Most of the conversations in this book first appeared, often in a slightly shorter version, in *Ventana.* Some were published in *El Nuevo Amanecer Cultural* [*Cultural New Dawn*], the literary supplement of the independent daily, *El Nuevo Diario.* A few are published here for the first time.

I soon began to see the series, in the light of my original exchange with Jack, as a way to explore the creative process in a place where the daily reality is one of extreme social upheaval (and where the most creative members of society are at the same time those who take responsibility for, and carry, its excruciating daily workload). In a more general sense, I thought, such a book might open new windows on the relationship between society and artistic expression in Nicaragua. And, for North American readers, it would provide a look at the passions and sensitivity, the history and ideas, the creativity and expression of these men and women who move between the dream world and the real world, shaping both simultaneously.

Not all of Nicaragua's political leadership are poets, of course. Nor do all poets in Nicaragua hold government or party posts. Yet the overlap is impressive. Of the three members of the country's Government Junta, Sergio Ramírez is an outstanding novelist whose books have been translated into a dozen languages. Daniel Ortega is a fine poet.

Among the nine members of the FSLN's National Directorate, we can add the writings of Tomás Borge and Jaime Wheelock to those of Ortega. Poetry in verse and prose, children's stories, and incisive sociological and historical essays give a broader and more profound dimension to the individual voices within the collective, which is basically articulated in speeches and conferences by all nine leaders.

One of Latin America's most important living poets (perhaps one of the most important poets writing in the Spanish language) is Ernesto Cardenal, Nicaragua's Minister of Culture. Gioconda Belli, author of the Casa de las Américas prize-winning book of poems, *Línea de frente* [*Front Line*], holds an important FSLN position. Other writers—such as Omar Cabezas, Dora María Téllez, Carlos Guadamuz, Rosario Murillo, Lizandro Chávez Alfaro, Francisco de Asís Fernández, and Vidaluz Menéses—hold key posts in this society being recreated from its roots.

These poets, these writers, were involved in the battle to overthrow Somoza. Some of them led that battle. Others participated to varying degrees, each according to individual commitment, degree of courage, organizational links to the FSLN, and other factors. In the following pages are conversations with writers who spent years underground or in prison; who came to know the rough mountains of the north from months in guerrilla camps; who operated clandestine radios, wrote propaganda, hid people in their homes, or organized civic opposition to the dictatorship.

Interestingly, among the truly important Nicaraguan writers, today there is only one—Pablo Antonio Cuadra, coeditor of *La Prensa*[2]—who does not support the revolutionary process. All the rest are involved—some engaged in positions of responsibility, while others simply enjoy the breathing and writing space finally opened up through a people's victory.

The great number of writers, principally poets, in Nicaragua could easily have made for a book twice as long as this one, or for several such books. I want to say right here that the collec-

---

2. *La Prensa* was for years the newspaper of the bourgeois opposition in Nicaragua. After the victory it moved quickly to the right, and in May of 1980 approximately 85 percent of those working on it quit to found *El Nuevo Diario*. *La Prensa* today represents the voice of counterrevolution inside the country.

tion is partial, and in some ways responds to my somewhat arbitrary choices. Among those absent from this volume there is one whose name I feel obliged to mention: Carlos Martínez Rivas. Carlos Martínez is certainly one of the great voices of Nicaraguan twentieth-century literature, and his exclusion from this collection is one I sincerely regret. Ernesto Mejía Sánchez, the important Nicaraguan poet living (for the most part) in Mexico, is another whose ideas would have been meaningful here. José Coronel Urtecho is one more extremely important poet. In his case, I didn't feel a conversation could have added anything to Manlio Tirado's excellent book-length interview, *Conversando con José Coronel Urtecho* [*Talking with José Coronel Urtecho*].[3]

There is also the whole matter of the Atlantic Coast. Nicaragua's two easternmost departments, Zelaya Norte and Zelaya Sur, were colonized by the English and became secondary stations for the Caribbean slave trade. The area developed very differently from the western part of the country. It is inhabited by Blacks, Creoles, and several native groups. Its cultural history has grown in English, Miskitu, and Sumo (these last two are native languages). All have produced a rich oral tradition, and there are outstanding poets in both the oral and written traditions. Among the English-language poets, David Macfield is to me the most interesting. However, he is currently Nicaragua's ambassador in Maputo, and it proved impossible to interview him in time for this book.

What has happened to Nicaraguan poetry and to literature in general? How have tradition and recent experience merged to push literary expression in one direction or another?

Most of those interviewed here speak of their links to Darío. His work is at the very roots of poetic experience in the country

3. Editorial Nueva Nicaragua, Managua, 1983.

in much the same way that Whitman's *Leaves of Grass* shaped poetry in the United States. As in most countries, there was a period of discovery of the Nicaraguan vernacular, and patterns of people's speech became important elements as did the country's rich folklore. José Coronel Urtecho and Ernesto Cardenal discovered and translated North American poetry (Pound, Williams, Dickinson) in the fifties, and the anthology that resulted from their collaboration was important both to them and to the poets who came after them.

Among the living poets, Cardenal has without a doubt exercised the greatest influence. His open, conversational style (which he has called *exteriorismo,* the voice of the everyday, of the real objects about us) has had an impact upon hundreds to whom his verse has been meaningful, and now—through the poetry workshops conducted by the Ministry of Culture—the influence has become institutionalized to a certain extent. César Vallejo and Pablo Neruda have been important to Nicaraguan poets, but that is true of Latin American poetry generally.

Perhaps the most interesting development in Nicaraguan literature, and one which has had a conscious boost from the revolution, has been the attention to oral history, the testimony of life in the words of those who live it; in poetry as well as in prose. In many ways this is an extension of Cardenal's *exteriorismo,* where people's voices are always a strong presence. But it also comes from the tremendous shared experience of clandestinity and war. Extraordinary emotions and deeds become one's daily reality. Already there are memoirs and diaries by some of the combatants (Germán Pomares's war diary; Borge's *Carlos, Dawn Is No Longer beyond Our Reach*; and Cabezas's *The Mountain Is More than Just a Great Expanse of Green* are the most important examples.)[4] Testimonial literature, although examples of it can be found in all languages and in all

4. Pomares's diary was partially published in *Nicarauac* No. 2. An English version of Borge's book is available through New Star Press, Vancouver, B.C. Cabezas's book, which won the 1982 Casa de las Américas award in the testimony category, will also soon be available to an English-reading public.

times, has been particularly important in Latin America during
the last twenty-five years, and is directly linked to the first
successful people's revolutions on the continent. The Nicaraguan experience is simply another chapter in this quarter-cen-
tury evolution.

During the literacy campaign in 1980, the brigadists teaching
reading and writing also recorded the life stories of many of the
peasants they taught. Thouands of these tapes exist in the archives of the Institute for the Study of Sandinism. They are a
valuable patrimony, and one day when time and resources
make it possible, a great people's literature will be extracted
from at least some of the stories. Even in the current situation,
there is a deep consciousness of the importance of preserving
the voices of the old Sandinistas (those who fought in the twen-
ties and thirties with General Sandino). The younger people are
also aware that their own story is worth telling. The Ministries
of Culture, Education, Agricultural Development, and the
Interior all conduct programs through which those interested
may learn the techniques of oral history.

It is too soon, perhaps, to speak of "a literature of the revolution," and in any case it is a complex subject requiring much
more space than I want to take here. Suffice, for these notes, to
say that the literature beginning to emerge from these dramatic
years is one rooted heavily in a people's search for their authentic origins; it is a literature involving highly individualized
visions of a collective voice, and at the same time, it uses the *real
maravilloso* (sometimes called "magical realism," that seemingly
surreal version of reality, which is real only to those who know
that in Latin America the apparently "unreal" is daily
experience).

It's important, as well, to speak—however briefly—of the role
of women in the fabric of this new poetic voice. Among the
finest and most prolific of Nicaraguan poets today are a number
of women: Michele Najlis, Vidaluz Menéses, Gioconda Belli,
Daisy Zamora, Rosario Murillo, Ana Ilce Gómez, Maríantonia
Henríquez, Olivia Silva, among others. Some of them speak in
the pages of this book. Although there have been women poets
in Nicaragua's earlier history (Mariana Sansón Arguello and

others), they have never appeared in such numbers nor with such strength. This, of course, has to do with the role women have played in recent years in the society as a whole.

From the beginning, the Sandinistas have been emphatically clear about the need for absolute artistic freedom in the new Nicaragua. The usual discussions have taken place, in which those favoring some form of socialist realism tangle with those intent on preserving a broader concept of the creative terrain. The results of these open polemics have simply served to strengthen the Nicaraguan conviction that "the role of the writer in the revolution is, first of all," in Tomás Borge's words, "to write well . . . We cannot put all these human creative possibilities inside a narrow circle in the name of a temporal slogan. It would be like trapping them in the circles of hell . . . Writers must be allowed to grow their own wings so they can fly to whatever heights they please."

This is, of course, Tomás Borge speaking more as a political leader than as a writer. As a political leader he is concerned with the role of writers vis-à-vis the political process. Perhaps, in this respect, what men and women whose primary activity is writing have to say about all this is more to the point (because it emerges from a daily praxis, in which the contradictions are every bit as great as the freedom). A search for as many different answers as there were writers interviewed became a constant preoccupation during the making of this book.

The Nicaraguan Revolution has provided much more than simply a context for the expression of these ideas. In spite of necessary priorities, the new state has placed strategic importance on, and given great resources to, cultural work. Less than a week after the 1979 victory, the mansion of Somoza's wife was turned into the country's first Ministry of Culture. (In all of Latin America, there are only two other countries that have raised cultural matters to a ministerial level, Cuba and Costa Rica.)

Father Ernesto Cardenal—he discusses the subject in this book—was asked to be Minister of Culture. He was not only a great poet, but he had the experience of his contemplative community at Solentiname behind him; there, many formerly marginalized peasants had taken up poetry, painting, and crafts. Cardenal was asked to extend to the entire nation his island vision of a people's creativity.

One of the ministry's pet projects has been the poetry workshops that are now active in countryside and cities, involving factory workers, peasants, policemen, students, housewives, and soldiers. The richness of the experience prompted Cardenal, in a 1982 address at Harvard University, to claim, "Our army can offer advisers to any army in the world—in matters relating to poetry!"

The Ministry of Culture also sponsors a fine international literary quarterly, *Nicarauac;* a smaller, more spontaneous poetry journal, *Poesía Libre;* and the magazine that prints work by those beginners who frequent the People's Culture Houses around the country, *Chacalaca.* Its literature department fills the Edgard Mungía Experimental Theater on the third Tuesday of each month with readings that have become a standard feature of Managua's cultural life; and poets and listeners from all over the country gather at Ciudad Darío (Darío City) on January 18th of each year. Darío's birthdate has been used to promote a new tradition in which hundreds join in a marathon reading lasting from early morning to sundown.

The Sandinista Cultural Workers Association (ASTC) was established to house a series of unions—among them, the Writers Union—through which professional artists may exchange ideas, learn from one another, teach, read, promote their work, publish, travel, and attempt collectively to solve work-related problems. In short, ASTC artists participate with their art in the daily life of the society that they are helping to mold. The unions are a unique experiment because they are an effort toward linking the idea of the writers and artists unions of the socialist countries (basically professional associations) with the capitalist countries' trade union concept (in which copyright, retirement, and other social benefits are contemplated).

Some of the contradictions still inherent in the lives of artists and writers in the new Nicaragua can be seen by taking a look at how these unions have functioned in the two years or so that they've existed. Some have clearly been much more effective than others. The theater people, dancers, and musicians have struggled through all sorts of problems, but they have strong unions. So do the painters. The basic reason seems to be the fact that all these people see their union as their fundamental link to society. An impressively large number of Nicaraguan painters work in their studios at home, and their union is—literally—their marketplace, where they share ideas, bring their paintings, sell them, and arrange shows.

Musicians—especially many of the older ones who have struggled for years in marching bands or in commercial trios and who have played on streetcorners or in barns—are for the first time being financially sponsored on a steady basis and getting retirement pensions—through their union. The same is true of the circus artists, men and women who didn't even qualify as members of the working class during the Somoza regime. Dance and theater groups organize their workshops and schedule their performances through the union structure. What all this means, of course, is that these people *need* their union; it is their active link with what's going on around them, and a way for them to be part of that. If they want to join the People's Militia, if they want to take a first aid course (widespread now, with the threat of invasion), if they want to volunteer to pick coffee or cotton or to enroll in an adult education course, it's the union that arranges for all that.

But what of the writer? The Writers Union has been much less successful than the others, and ASTC people as well as some of the writers themselves have been interested in trying to understand why. Nicaraguan writers overwhelmingly took part in the insurrectional process. Why, then, have they had such difficulty in consolidating an active union? The main answer seems to lie in the fact that these men and women *are* actively involved in the nation's problems and solutions, but not necessarily through their union. Most have important positions in government or in the FSLN (as we've seen). If they enter the militia, go to pick coffee, or give classes in one skill or another, they do so through their workplace or with their neighborhood organization. The union is still secondary in their lives.

Through the ASTC, writers—as well as musicians, painters, sculptors, graphics people, dancers, photographers, circus artists, actors and theater people in general—have formed brigades and gone to the front lines in the war that is still being imposed daily on this wounded and determined people. This activity, central to the lives of numerous writers beginning in mid-1982, has had a profound effect on their work.

It's important to stop and talk a moment about these brigades, for I think they say a great deal about the new relationship being forged between cultural workers and the daily life of the nation. Contingents of four or five brigades, each with some twenty to twenty-five members, have gone out simultaneously, traveling for periods of two to three weeks, to the frontline combat posts of Sandinista soldiers and militia in the north, along the southern border, and on the Atlantic Coast. Each brigade includes one or two poets, a photographer, a painter interested in doing quick sketches of people and places, perhaps a small theater or folkloric dance group, a troupe of musicians, and a couple of circus clowns or jugglers.

These men and women have had the usual defensive militia training that most Nicaraguans undergo in a voluntary effort to prepare for armed aggression. But they aren't, for the most part, trained soldiers. They are old and young; established artists as well as beginners. Yet the brigade experiences bear little if any resemblance to the "Bob Hope entertaining the troops" idea so prevalent in "modern warfare." The ASTC brigadists go to the front lines, where they know they will be sharing the difficult living conditions with the soldiers, and most of all they know they will be sharing the danger.

I remember speaking to a member of the Pancasán Music Group about his recent experience on one of the brigades in the north, close to the Honduran border. "In eight days of work," he said, "we were able to give nine full performances. But there were times when we found ourselves singing under veritable crossfire. And other times when all the soldiers had to go into combat and we were the only ones left defending the camp." It's easy to see how this kind of experience must have a deep influence on the work of the artists and writers who take part. But there have been other by-products as well. Oral testimony from combatants has been recorded; collective journals have been kept; and occasionally some of the peasants, workers, or students turned soldiers have produced poems or songs of their own, which have then formed part of the collection of people's creativity gathered by the professional artists. I don't believe it's an exaggeration to say that several years of this work may produce a whole new (if incipient) literature.

There are a variety of publishing endeavors in Nicaragua, in spite of the shortages of all kinds (in paper, machinery, and parts, for example) common to the developing world and even more scarce in nations where other kinds of needs become priority. The universities in Managua and León each have their publication program. So do the Ministries of Culture and Education, as well as CIERA (the Agrarian Reform Research Center). There are also several private and religious publishing houses. But the most important is the state-owned Editorial Nueva Nicaragua, with its ambitious series of collections including one dedicated to Nicaragua's younger as well as more established writers.

This is particularly important in a country where publishing under the dictatorship was limited to the small, privately circulated editions financed by the poets themselves. And customs censorship during the Somoza regime kept out most modern thought and literature. Commander Doris Tijerino, in a book about her life,[5] tells how Marx's *The Sacred Family* once got by customs because the official thought it was a religious book. And Ernesto Cardenal, whose island community in the sixties and seventies was very close to the Costa Rican border, has often spoken of the booklists customs officials used in order to determine what literature would be allowed into the country and what wouldn't. During the Somoza regime, many Latin

---

5. *Doris Tijerino: Inside the Nicaraguan Revolution,* as told to Margaret Randall, New Star Books, Vancouver, B.C., Canada, 1978.

American writers prided themselves on being on those lists. A book didn't have to be narrowly political to be kept out. Sartre, Dostoyevsky, Camus, Julio Cortázar, and Cardenal himself were all prohibited.

Nicaragua is a small Central American nation, with fewer than three million people. Worse than being simply a "banana republic" in the eyes of the United States, the country's geopolitical situation (which poses the possibility of building a second interoceanic canal) justified constant control and supervision. There is even a North American president in Nicaragua's history (William Walker, 1858–60). Finally the U.S. engineered the murder, in 1934, of General Augusto César Sandino, the only man able to oust the Marine Corps. And the United States installed the first Somoza with a National Guard capable of keeping him—and U.S. interests—in power by force of arms. Through a succession of fathers, uncles, and sons, the Somoza family ruled for close to half a century. Sandino's heirs, the Sandinistas, waged a twenty-year struggle that finally toppled the dictator in 1979.

Numerous writers and poets took part in that struggle. Some are martyrs to its cause. Ricardo Morales, university professor turned Sandinista and gunned down in 1973, left important essays and poems, which have been collected since his death. Arlen Siu, killed in combat in 1975, had poems and songs to her credit. Fernando Gordillo, Sandinista student leader, died in 1967, and the Cultural House which also holds the offices of the ASTC in Managua bears his name. But perhaps the outstanding poet, whose great visionary talent was cut short by an early death, is Leonel Rugama.[6]

6. Sara Miles and Richard Schaaf are currently translating Rugama's complete poetry into English, and Curbstone Press in Wilimantic, Connecticut, is planning a near-future publication.

Rugama was from the northern city of Estelí. Something of
his youth comes through here in the interview with Omar
Cabezas. He was an exceptional poet and a man who knew
early that his life would be given over to the struggle to free
Nicaragua. He was not yet twenty-one years old when hundreds
of National Guardsmen surrounded the house where he and
two others were caught on January 15th, 1970. The battle
lasted several hours, and the forces of "law and order" em-
ployed tanks and a helicopter against the three young men.
When the head of the attacking force picked up a megaphone
and shouted *"Qué se rinde!"* into the smoking house, Rugama,
who was the last of the three alive, replied, *"Qué se rinde tu
madre!"* An accurate translation might be "Surrender!" followed
by "Up yours!" *"Qué se rinde tu madre!"* has become the official
slogan for Nicaragua's cultural workers. At mass demonstrations, workers from the Ministry of Culture can be seen marching behind great banners with those words written across them.
It is a way of honoring this quiet, dedicated ex-seminary student
become Sandinista fighter, who, throughout his years at the
university in Léon, often showed his poems to friends, claiming
they had been written by his brother, "a shy kid who likes to
write . . ."

What is the relationship between struggle and creativity in the
new Nicaragua? Border incursions, sabotage, and bombings by
U.S.-backed ex-Somoza people have taken several thousand
lives since 1979. Continued attack means the need for continued resistance. Writers and artists, along with their brothers
and sisters in other areas of activity, must dedicate themselves
first to keeping their revolution alive, to preserving the peace.
The overwhelming majority of Nicaraguan writers fought for
this revolution, believe in it, and know that only through its
consolidation can they really achieve the freedom and peace of
mind necessary to sustained creativity.

But this makes for some obvious contradictions. The institutions of the revolution have seen cultural activity and creativity as *necessary* to the task of preserving authentic tradition and values as well as to a people's growth and to changing an oppressive value system. The revolution has *designed* a real people's participation in cultural expression (ranging from the support given to established artists to programs aimed at ordinary people—peasants, workers, students, housewives, children—who simply feel the need to articulate their creativity). The priority tasks are so consuming at this point that there is, first of all, *little physical time in which to work.*

Sergio Ramírez, who dedicates himself almost exclusively to the tasks of head of state, accepts the fact that the coming years will see the expression of his ideas reduced to public addresses, papers, and essays. Ernesto Cardenal, who has often spoken of his dream of retiring to Solentiname where he would "chronicle the revolution," was asked on a recent U.S. tour how he writes poems while attending to his duties as Minister of Culture. He replied, "I write short ones." Gioconda Belli, who has been one of the more prolific poets in Nicaragua's recent history (several of her new poems have been set to music and have become familiar songs to hundreds of thousands of Nicaraguans) has oscillated between continuing to be a public poet and stating her belief that this moment in time requires a temporary sacrifice in that respect. Daisy Zamora goes deeper than others, perhaps, in her discussion of this difficult problem for many of the country's top writers.

These conversations are with a number of men and women who rank with the best writers currently exercising their craft in the Spanish language (Cardenal, Ramírez, Belli, Chávez Alfaro). Some of those interviewed are writers first, and secondly architects of the new society (Valle-Castillo, Najlis, Menéses, Morales, Blandón, Zamora). Others are the real Sandinista poets, those political and military leaders about whom one is surprised to learn a writer coexists in the same skin (Tomás Borge, Omar Cabezas, Carlos Guadamuz, Francisco de Asís Fernández). Those who are writers first explore their feelings and their experiences with the creative process and its insertion in this historic period. Commander Tomás Borge, who is clearly only a writer in one of his many facets, nevertheless speaks out of a poet's sensibility when he addresses the needs of creative people in a revolutionary situation, the need of the revolution for creative people, and what the revolution's attitude toward these people must be.

Here are their voices, recorded throughout 1983 in Managua. Here, too, is some of their work, as well as photographic images which will help bring each poet into focus. In one way or another, all these men and women are the guerrilla poets of a heretofore unpublished experience.

MARGARET RANDALL
Albuquerque
January 1984

Sergio Ramírez

There's a centrifugal force here

To say it's a country of poets is more than a commonplace when speaking of Nicaragua. Perhaps, and particularly at this time, it denotes something as complex as it is beautiful. Often, when the international news agencies come forth with their distorted images of the leadership of the Sandinista People's Revolution, one feels like responding by speaking of the "guerrilla poets": men and women—many of them extraordinary poets, essayists, and novelists—who because of their commitment to their country have had to put aside temporarily their writer's pen and allow themselves full expression, at least for the moment, only in the public speech, conference, or talk.

The problems of the writer in the context of a threatened revolution is a topic of debate in today's Nicaragua. If one is a writer, and at the same time part of the country's high-level leadership, the choices, the contradictions, and the problems themselves become sharper. But perhaps, at the same time, simpler. This was some of what was running through my mind as I sat in his outer office, waiting for Sergio Ramírez—member of the Government Junta and of the Sandinista Assembly, as well as an exceptional novelist—to receive me.

Sergio Ramírez of *Tiempo de fulgor (Time of Brightness)* and *Te dio miedo la sangre?* [*Were You Frightened of the Blood?*]. Later,

Sergio Ramírez of "The Twelve."[1] And today, Sergio Ramírez of the brilliant speeches, in his office at Government House, and in his weekly appearances on "Meet the People."[2] When I'd requested the interview I imagined I'd have to wait weeks. And I was surprised when, a few days later, there I was waiting for a conversation which would be far from the last appointment of the day for him.

Here, then, with a minimum of editing, are his words.

Sergio: I was born in Masatepe. I come from a petit bourgeois family—my father was a farmer, my mother a school teacher—and I grew up in a small town in the state of Masaya, a place with very little which might have stimulated a literary life. Nor was there anything in my childhood that smacked of literature, except in the sense that any child has a series of experiences which, later, may be drawn on for literary purposes, if the person has a gift for that.

I finished the early part of my secondary education there in Masatepe. Then I studied with the Christian Brothers for a while, in Diriamba and Managua. And later I went on to the university at León.

That move from Masatepe to León was very important in my life: going from such a small town to the big city, where the university was. And that was a decisive period, of course, for me as well as for the country as a whole. It was 1959, and the Cuban Revolution had triumphed. A new stage had begun for Latin America. In Nicaragua, even the bourgeoisie thought it was possible to defeat the dictatorship through the force of arms.

My entrance into the university meant a radical change for me as well, because I came from a family that had always been

1. "The Twelve" refers to a group of well-known figures from Nicaraguan life—priests, writers, men of finance, university professors, and lawyers—who got together in 1978 and openly supported the FSLN's armed struggle to overthrow Somoza.

2. "Meet the People" is a weekly televised meeting between Nicaragua's highest government officials and the people in a given neighborhood, at a factory, peasant base, etc. Problems are aired in frank discussion; explanations are given and solutions are sought.

affiliated with Somoza's Liberal Party. Both my mother's and my father's sides of the family had supported the Liberals from the time they took power in 1927. We can't forget that Moncada[3] was from Masatepe: he was the only president ever to have come from that town. The businessmen, the small land owners, and the few aristocrats in the place: none of them thought of Moncada as a traitor. They simply thought of him as the only president Masatepe ever gave the country, a president who wasn't from León or from Granada—for a change—and

3. José María Moncada (1868–1945) was president of Nicaragua from 1929 to 1932. He opposed Sandino, and when faced with U.S. intervention in 1932 he declared martial law.·

they remembered that Moncada had brought electricity and drinking water to the town. Despite the fact that these were Moncada's private enterprises, they were seen as the president's public works.

My father was mayor of Masatepe in the fifties, and he even took up a public collection to erect a monument to Moncada; it was in the central square and it was the only monument in town. So Moncada's presence was important. And the Liberal Party was important in and of itself, for as my maternal grandmother used to say, the Liberals were the ones who put an end to the Conservative Party practice of coming armed in the middle of the night to the homes of the Liberals in the area, and taking them off to fight on the Conservative side in the civil wars before 1927. For her, for my grandmother, Somoza meant stability: the Liberal Party in power. And you can't underestimate the figure of Moncada in all that.

All of this in spite of the fact that Sandino was from Niquihonomo, the same general area, just a few miles from Masatepe. And Sandino was even related by blood to my father's family; my grandmother was a sister of América Sandino. And they were close. But Sandino was like a curse. As I grew up, Sandino was nothing more to me than the way he was portrayed in Somoza's book, *The Calvary of the Segovias;* that was our only source of "information" about the hero. Sandino was the one who beheaded, murdered, and raped the Segovias—according to that vision—while Moncada was the great public personage. Sandino was the dark, mysterious figure, about whom one could not speak with pride.

And just to complete the triangle, we might mention that Somoza himself had been born in San Marcos. Again, the same area. On a quiet day one can hear the church bells of one of those towns in any of the others, or the sounds of the fireworks in the celebration of patron saints. Somoza was governor of San Marcos when he became president of the republic. He lived right there, he had power, and he was the Liberal Party personified. So when I left Masatepe, at the age of seventeen, my political view was in no way that of an anti-Somoza person.

You have to understand all this in order to understand what a shock it was for me to enter the university, there at León. My father planned on my being a lawyer. I went to study law because that was my father's decision. For him, the most important thing I could do was to study law and open an office right there in our home town of Masatepe. And I was the first member of the whole huge Ramírez family who was to graduate in law. A family in which I had fifty-six cousins and almost twenty aunts and uncles, on my paternal and maternal sides. So you can imagine how important it was to my father that I get my degree in law. It was one of the dreams of his life. I was his oldest son.

And so I arrived in León. And I simply had no choice but to study law. Looking back, perhaps I might have enjoyed studying something else, literature perhaps, or architecture. But it was predetermined. And, in this context, the changes I underwent at the university were very important to me.

As I said, I entered the university at a time when all of Latin America was beginning to feel the political impact of the Cuban Revolution. For me, and in my hometown, the Cuban Revolution was the "26th of July" anthem sung by Daniel Santos on the jukebox, and red and black flags in the trees and flying from the bell tower on the church. I didn't really understand what had happened in Cuba until I got to the university.

At the university I was suddenly in a new environment. The traditional school was breaking out of its shell through a series of internal reforms being made at that time. The university had gained its autonomy in 1957. That autonomy was ratified in 1958, and that meant a lot of educational renovation. Above all, there was the influence of the president of the school, Dr. Mariano Fiallos Gil, who was a key figure in the ideological, political, and cultural formation of what would later be known as the Autonomy Generation. And beyond those two things—the Cuban Revolution and the movement for university autonomy—we felt the impact, as well (and for me it was a very direct impact), of the struggle going on in the streets, the struggle, the student demonstrations, against the dictatorship.

The landing at Olama and Los Mollejones[4] coincided with my arrival at the university, and that put an end to classes, automatically. We went back to receive yet another shock: the massacre at El Chaparral.[5] I remember the demonstrations in the street in front of La Merced Church, where for the first time I climbed up on a desk and made a political speech. I was protesting the death of Carlos Fonseca, because we initially heard that Carlos had been killed in the massacre at El Chaparral.

All you heard in the streets were cries about the assassination of Carlos, and that led to a series of demonstrations throughout the last week of June and the first two weeks of July. Requiem masses were held at El Calvario Church; there were demonstrations along the main street; women gathered in the market; workers gathered as well. It was a permanent atmosphere of agitation. Everyday there were clashes with the Guard. Tear gas bombs. And it all came to a head on July 23rd, when the Guard fired on a freshman demonstration (it was a traditional frosh parade which usually carried with it a great deal of clowning around, but that year we held it without any clowning at all—to protest the El Chaparral massacre—we all wore white shirts and black ties and the women wore solid black, in sign of mourning). That demonstration was repressed by the Guard, as I say, and four compañeros were killed. Two of them were in first-year law with me: Mauricio Martínez and Erick Ramírez. We had entered the university together.

I myself was a survivor of that massacre. I was there when the Guard opened fire, and I helped take the wounded to a hospital; I saw the dead lying in the street. All that had a tremendous impact on my life. It was probably the most decisive event up to that time. It changed my political and ideological criteria completely, as well as how I saw my future.

For me it meant a radical change, for me and for many others who were there and had some level of political involvement,

4. Landing by a group of bourgeoisie opposition to Somoza, including Pedro Joaquín Chamorro. They were captured.
5. First guerrilla action by some of those who would later make up the initial nucleus of the FSLN. They were defeated in battle.

like Fernando Gordillo, who had been at the university since 1958. Fernando came from the Pedagogical Institute; not like me. I came from a public school in the provinces. He came from Managua and was a leader among the students, a good speaker, well known as a speaker. He'd won oratory contests at the university by that time, and we could say he was one of the main leaders in spite of his youth. And others: Joaquín Solis Piura, president of the CUUN [University of Nicaragua Student Center] then. Luís Felipe Pérez Caldera, Humberto Obregón, Tito Castillo; they were part of that whole movement that later erupted into the events at the university. And I especially want to mention Manolo Morales.

After the July 23rd massacre classes stopped again, and when they reopened in September, a struggle took place in which I had an active participation. It was to expel the military personnel studying at the school. There were even some soldiers in my first-year law classes. First, we staged a sit-in, the first to be held at a public institution, and then we took over the university. After a hunger strike in which Manolo Morales participated, we held an assembly and decided to simply stay there. We locked ourselves in, until we could get the military expelled from campus. The Guard surrounded us and there was a lot of tension. But we finally won; Somoza decided to remove the military and send them to foreign universities to study, especially to Spain. So that was a battle won.

So the 23rd of July, 1959, was what consolidated the political formation of what would later be known as the Autonomy Generation. And we must include in that generation Carlos Fonseca, Tomás Borge, Silvio Mayorga—who had been at the university since 1957, although I didn't meet them then because Carlos was involved in the armed actions at El Chaparral and Tomás was in exile. By the time the 23rd of July came along they weren't physically present, but they were definitely among the founders of all those movements launched by the Autonomy Generation, which was later to develop into the New Nicaragua Movement in the early sixties. And later became "Patriotic Youth." All this in the context of the great expectations raised by the Cuban Revolution and the Algerian liberation struggle; leading up to the founding of the Sandinista National Liberation Front.

It was within that political context that the *Ventana* literary movement surfaced in 1960; it was a literary and cultural expression of the whole movement of the Autonomy Generation.

I think that was about the time I began writing my first poems. Before I decided to stick to narrative. When I began writing short stories it was with quite a traditional approach, along the lines of the concept of folk tales published by *La Prensa Literaria*, the most accessible medium for me at that time. In those years my friendship with Juan Aburto was very meaningful to me. I had visited him since I got to the university, whenever I came here to Managua. His office was in what was then the National Bank Building. He had a small library at home as well; I remember having permanent access to a bookcase with glass doors. So I was able to read North American writers like Hart Crane, O'Henry—writers I'd never heard of before. And they offered a new perspective, different from that of the vernacular narrative. I began writing my first stories in 1960 or '61.

But speaking of *Ventana*, it was a poor magazine we published, but its perspectives were extraordinary. As I said, the first issue came out in June of 1960. I got the idea for the magazine during my summer vacation in Masatepe that year. I wrote to Fernando, suggesting the idea for a cultural publication—of course it didn't have a name yet—and I also wrote to several of my friends at the university who had cultural or literary leanings. I sent them a collective letter, saying we should launch a magazine. No one answered, until one day Fernando Gordillo showed up in Masatepe—that was in March of 1960. He showed up with his father's car, and with Manolo Morales. And they came just to talk about the idea of the magazine. The decision to go through with the project was made that afternoon in Masatepe, with Manolo and Fernando. I went to speak with Dr. Fiallos Gil, to see if the university would be willing to finance it. He promised to pay the printer as long as we promised to get advertising from businesses there in León. Then we began looking for a name.

Fernando insisted I be the director, since it was my idea. But I convinced him it should be both of us, and so we both appeared as directors from the first issue. I remember Fernando was actually in charge of that first issue, because I had to go to Guatemala in 1960 for a Central American Oratory Contest. The first cover shows a kind of cubist window formed by the letters of the word *ventana* (window) on a yellow background. It was a very simple cover, Fernando's idea. That first issue had twelve pages, standard-bond paper. We printed five hundred copies at the Christian Brothers print shop. That was how the thing was born.

Everything new that was happening at the time was published in *Ventana*. And from the beginning, we controlled the political vision, making sure the magazine put forth the line we were interested in. And it was a very important event on the Nicaraguan literary scene at the time. Because the most important literary influence then, the "pope of letters" you might say, was Pablo Antonio Cuadra. He ruled the world from the pages of *La Prensa Literaria*. And we all published there as well. But *La Prensa Literaria* virtually demanded that we be apolitical. Or, more accurately, rather than apolitical—because you could always publish a poem or two against Somoza there—it was a kind of ideological asepsis as far as literature went. That was what the reactionaries wanted of us. They didn't want us to contaminate literature with ideological questions. Although the Vanguard Movement had been founded, of course, with a fascist ideology—since that was the trend of the times.

When we began taking shots at that position of theirs, we were immediately accused of degenerating literature, of contaminating it, and we were told it was impossible to make good literature like that, with what was called committed prose or verse, an option that took into consideration the worker or the peasant; literature that involved social struggle. That couldn't really be literature! Real literature had to be beyond all that. So it was out of that contradiction that *Ventana*'s political position was born. And then there was the later polarization with what became known as the Betrayed Generation.

The Betrayed Generation, all of its members protégés of *La Prensa Literaria,* was headed by Edwin Illescas and Roberto Cuadra. It set itself up as a movement of young people who were out to salvage the purity of Nicaragua's quality literature. Quality, as they saw it, based on permanent experimentation and innovation. We were condemned for being politically committed, so of course we could contribute nothing new. We couldn't be innovators, in their eyes. The Betrayed Generation saw itself as called to nourish what they thought of as the great current of Nicaraguan literature.

Seen in the context of the class struggle in our country, the Betrayed Generation's ideological position seemed inoffensive. It was the Nicaraguan version of the "Beat Generation" and "The Angry Young Men" in vogue in the United States and England at that time, in the late fifties and early sixties, after the Korean War. It was represented by Jack Kerouac and Lawrence Ferlinghetti, all those poets we knew through *El Corno Emplumado* . . . existential angst in the face of the consumer society and the asphalt jungle.

Here it was something else. It was a matter of building a political position antithetical to ours, that is, a call to the existence of the individual and for individuality destroyed by a mass consumer society. So as not to look at Nicaragua's real problems. Looking at it now, in retrospect and with the clarity that comes with time, it was a colonialist import of concerns alien to our reality, which we now call by its real name: diversionism. Imported under the guise of a shining halo, making a "new" literature, introducing new literary and cultural forms and content into our literature here in Nicaragua. That was always true of literature, of course, but now it included an alienating ideological content. The Betrayed Generation accused us of impoverishing literature with themes which were too prosaic.

It was about that time that the political and ideological struggle between the *Ventana* movement, on the one hand, and the Betrayed Generation, on the other, was organized. We debated these topics publicly in the magazines: we from the pages of *Ventana,* and the Betrayed Generation from the pages of *La Prensa Literaria.* We even held a congress of poets and writers, organized by *Ventana* in León. We invited all the groups: the Betrayed Generation; a group that existed in Boaco, the "U" Group, headed by Flavio Tijerino and Armando Incer. It was October of 1961, if I'm not mistaken. Fernando Gordillo was already very ill by that time. He was in a hospital in Mexico, and couldn't come.

There was a certain legitimacy to importing literature here in Nicaragua. A tradition. Something that had always taken place. We had always imported North American literature, from the Vanguard Movement, with Coronel Urtecho, to the Post-Vanguard, with Ernesto Cardenal. North American literature had contributed enormously to the modernization of Nicaraguan literature, to the creation of a new and dynamic poetry here. That's obvious. We don't deny the innovative importance of that literature. And we published it consistently in *Ventana*. We never followed a closed policy, or refused to publish those poets in our magazine. We published them, but with our own critical position as well. And that was the real scandal for the Right. On the second anniversary of the Cuban Revolution, we published Cuban poetry. And when we published North American poetry from the anthology being prepared at that time by Cardenal and Coronel, we chose that which we felt had the most social commitment because it reflected the reality we ourselves wanted to emphasize: the North American poor oppressed by capitalism.

Around that time I joined the FER, the Revolutionary Student Front, founded in 1961–if I'm not mistaken–here in Managua. I took part in the constitutional assembly of the FER, in the old school of economics, near El Triunfo Street in the San Sebastián area of the city. Once we had the FER going, we made up platforms for student council elections and began winning them year after year, already with the perspective of a revolutionary organization.

In 1962 I met with Carlos Fonseca in León, at Sergio Martínez's house. He was underground and hiding out there. We talked about *Ventana*. I remember he held a few issues in his hand while he explained to me the magazine's political importance in the perspective of revolutionary struggle, and why we had to keep a clear line with it.

I continued to participate in the FER, but I didn't yet belong to the Sandinista National Liberation Front during my university years. I should say that being a member of the FSLN at that time meant living underground. You couldn't be a member and keep living a normal life. You had to opt for clandestinity and absolute sacrifice. Very few members from those years survived and are alive today. I'm not one of them.

I left the university in 1964, and Carlos Tunnerman,[6] who was in Costa Rica, offered me a job on the Central American University Council of Higher Education (CSUCA). I accepted. I didn't open the law office my father wanted. Truthfully, in spite of the fact that I was a good student of law, I never really thought I would practice. And I was totally convinced of that by the time I left school. The law profession didn't interest me. By that time I wanted to be a writer, no matter what it took. When I left the university in 1964 I had already published my first book of short stories, and I was thinking of writing a novel. I thought I'd have better conditions for writing that novel in Costa Rica—that was *Tiempo de fulgor [Time of Brilliance]*—and I was right. I settled down to work on that novel and I finished it in 1966–67. Then I finished my second book of short stories, also in the sixties. The first was called *Stories,* the second *New Stories*. I worked on some of my most important stories then, among them "Charles Atlas Also Dies."

I mentioned Dr. Fiallos Gil before. He was an important figure in my life and in that of my generation. And in the life of the *Ventana* group. He was a man with a new kind of mentality, one we might now call progressive, liberal, cultured. He helped encourage our generation to have a critical and antidogmatic approach in its literary, cultural, and political concerns; to read everything, investigate everything. Little by little I grew closer to him until I ended up as a kind of private secretary to his office in my post of public relations person for the university.

I went to Costa Rica when Fiallos Gil was already very ill. He died in September, I think, of 1964, a few months after I left

6. Carlos Tunnerman was later one of "The Twelve," and with the Sandinista victory he became Minister of Education, a position he still holds.

Nicaragua. Then, since the elections were to be held in January of 1965 and Carlos Tunnerman became president of the university, he asked me to stay in Costa Rica to support CSUCA. I began to ascend the bureaucratic ladder until, in 1968, I became Secretary General of the organization. I held that position until 1973, when I went to Germany.

By then, as I mentioned before, I had two books of short stories published. And a third in the hands of Joaquín Mortiz.[7] And I had the novel, *Tiempo de fulgor.* At that point I felt more than ever that I had to be a writer. I was convinced, and I'm still convinced, that one can't be a writer unless one is completely dedicated to the craft, full time, a professional. And in 1967 I had met someone who was to be very important to me in my life as a writer: Peter Schultz-Kraft, a German who worked for the United Nations in El Salvador. We met in Costa Rica. He was interested in doing an anthology of Central American writers, to be published in Germany. We began a very deep friendship, which has continued to this day. He translated my first stories into German; he took an interest in my career as a writer and it was through him that I was able to obtain a scholarship in 1973 from the Berlin academic exchange program. The scholarship consisted of a monthly stipend for a year; one goes there and does nothing but write.

I stayed for two years, the first with the grant and the second with a teaching contract, thanks to Johannes Rau, now premier of Renania, one of the German states. There I finished my novel *¿Te dio miedo la sangre?* [*Were You Frightened of the Blood?*]. I also wrote "A Boy from Niquihonomo," which was originally the prologue to the German edition of *The Living Thought of Sandino.* Also the essay published recently by Siglo XXI, *Balconies and Volcanoes,* an interpretation of the cultural history of Central America, which is about to be published as well by the New Nicaraguan Press.

I also wrote a weekly column for *La Prensa Literaria,* a column called "Ventana," about cultural information, what I was experiencing in Germany: films, books, all sorts of things. So I was

7. An important Mexican publisher.

living as a professional writer, working from eight in the morning to six in the evening, at a typewriter, like any typist. By night I had the opportunity of getting a really thorough film education, in the movie houses of Berlin. That helped a lot to complete my vision as a writer. Film has always had a decisive influence in my work. And it's something I long for these days, because of course I see very little now. . . ."

It might seem like there's a leap in all this, but I never left politics. Between 1966 and '67 I was in very close contact with Carlos Fonseca once more, this time in Costa Rica. I met him again in August of 1966 and we saw each other frequently until November of that year, until he returned to Nicaragua. Those were the months prior to Pancasán.[8] And that permanent daily contact with Carlos, our conversations about so many topics, about the history of Nicaragua, about Rubén Darío (at that time he was doing research on Darío at the National Library in San José), that contact was important to me.

Without participating actively as a member of the FSLN, I was involved to some extent in all the difficulties following Carlos's arrest after Humberto Ortega's rescue attempt in Costa Rica. Then came the attack on Chema Castillo's house in December of 1974. That's another crucial event in this second part of my political development.

What happened? I went to Germany, having decided to be a writer, to write professionally, taking every advantage of the opportunities offered. But the taking of the Chema Castillo house had a profound effect on me. Because at that moment in time when I had the chance to stay in Europe—I was offered work in Paris, at the new Pompidou Center, which was about to open—I decided I had to return to Central America, to Nicaragua.

I decided to cut short what might have been my career as a writer because I felt that the FSLN was embarking on a new stage in struggle after the attack on Chema Castillo's house.

---

8. Pancasán, in 1967, was another defeat for the still incipient FSLN guerrilla movement. That is, it was a military defeat, in which much of the leadership of the organization was killed in ambush. But it was a political turning point, in that it showed armed struggle as the only viable means to defeat the dictator.

And that perception, taken in Europe, wasn't wrong. After that, I began a more active role. As a writer, I began to work on a propaganda task which later became important: it was the preparation of a listing of Somoza's properties, put together with a little information from Tino Pereira (then in Geneva working with the ILO), some of my own memories, and a bit of imagination, letters from friends, and other things.

Carlos Tunnerman was living in Washington then. He managed to get the listing to Jack Anderson, and when it was published it was a heavy blow for the dictatorship. Later, I went back to Costa Rica in 1975. I joined the FSLN in September, in their structure in Costa Rica, and they put me in charge of several tasks in propaganda and international information, including the preparation of the document Fernando Cardenal presented to the U.S. Congress denouncing the violation of human rights in Nicaragua. Luís Carrión and I prepared that document and we gave it to Fernando in Costa Rica.

Then I began to work in an underground propaganda structure for the solidarity committees, political tasks close to Humberto Ortega. I had previously had contact with Jaime Wheelock, since my university days (he was in charge of *Taller,* the continuation of *Ventana*), and I met Daniel when the Directorate put me in charge of organizing the Group of Twelve. That is to say, I met Humberto in January of 1976 and Daniel in March of 1977.

From 1976 on, I was practically a full-time political worker in the FSLN. I was reelected Secretary General of the CSUCA, but it was just a cover—I never really worked in that post again. The cover was useful for all sorts of political tasks, because CSUCA has diplomatic status in Costa Rica. In July of 1977 I went full time into the organization of the Group of Twelve.

That was one of the decisive steps taken with an eye toward consolidating political alliances, mobilizing all the social classes around the struggle against the dictatorship. It was an idea that took shape gradually in the minds of various leaders of the Front, an idea already put forth by Eduardo Contreras before he was assassinated in 1976. Later, it was up to Humberto and Daniel to give it impetus. After a meeting in Managua, which included Víctor, Daniel and Humberto, it was decided–as we all know–to move into an insurrectional offensive stage, which is what characterized that tendency of the FSLN, the Insurrectional Tendency.[9] Part of that was the political component of organizing a provisional government which, along with an insurrectional movement, would appear as the political head of a new government. That's how the Group of Twelve came about.

Fernando Cardenal,[10] who was actively participating in the FSLN, had already been contacted through the Front's internal structures. I was to recruit Miguel D'Escoto[11] in New York; I had been in touch with him because of Fernando's presentation to Congress. Also Tito Castillo,[12] in exile in Costa Rica, and Carlos Tunnerman, who was returning to Managua from Colombia where he worked as an advisor for UNESCO. Joaquín Cuadra, Sr.,[13] and Emilio Baltodano[14] were recruited inside the country. We held our first meeting in San José in late June 1977. There we met with Humberto Ortega. Felipe Mántica,[15] a member of the original group, was at that meeting.

We had a second meeting with the same people in Cuerna-vaca, Mexico, where the plan for a provisional government was approved. José Benito Escobar[16] was there representing the National Directorate. We met for three days to discuss the ap-

9. At the end of 1976, in the context of an urgent need for discussion around strategic and tactical aspects of the struggle, the FSLN split into three tendencies: Prolonged People's War, Proletarians, and Insurrectionals. The three groups came back to unified struggle in 1978.

10. Fernando Cardenal, Jesuit priest, member of "The Twelve," and member of the FSLN since the mid-seventies, headed the literacy campaign in 1980. Today he is on the national executive board of the Sandinista Youth Movement.

11. Miguel D'Escoto, a Maryknoll father, is Nicaragua's Minister of Foreign Affairs.

12. Ernesto (Tito) Castillo is a member of the Supreme Court.

13. Joaquín Cuadra, Sr., is Minister of Finances.

14. Emilio Baltodano is General Comptroller of the National Bank.

15. Felipe Mántica was a wealthy business magnate who was involved in the initial plans for a rebel government but later withdrew because of political differences.

16. José Benito Escobar was a member of the National Directorate of the FSLN, who was gunned down July 15, 1978, in Estelí. The Sandinista Trade Union Movement bears his name.

proval of the provisional government plan and the formation of said government—who would occupy the different positions. Some of those who later held government positions were decided on at that meeting in Cuernavaca.

Then, in October of 1977, when the military offensive didn't really come through, that group, which was prepared to enter the country as the new provisional government, decided to publish a manifesto. We came out with it on October 17th, and in it we publicly supported the struggle of the FSLN. The political impact was tremendous. For the first time in the history of Nicaragua a group of priests, businessmen, intellectuals, and professionals came out in support of the FSLN's armed struggle.

When they murdered Pedro Joaquín Chamorro,[17] we had arranged a meeting with him in Mexico; we'd arranged it through Edmundo Jarquín.[18] The purpose of the meeting was so that he could come to some kind of an agreement with the Twelve. I still have an inscription in a book Pedro Joaquín gave to me, in which he says, "From the probable number 13." I think that was his thinking at that time, and that he accepted the FSLN as something that had to be taken into account in the struggle against Somoza; he felt it was necessary to work with the Front, work with the organization which by that time clearly had the most weight and which was becoming, even for the bourgeoisie, the leading force against the dictatorship.

I practically hung up my gloves as a writer when I left Berlin, and returned to Nicaragua in 1975. I already had the final draft of my novel, and between September and December of 1975, while I became actively involved in working with the FSLN, I made the final corrections. I cut the stencil myself and I sent a copy off to the editors. With that, you might say, I stopped being a "professional writer."

Later, just before the victory, I wrote a screenplay for a film about Sandino. I think that was an important literary work, although I've never been able to go back and revise it, put it into

17.   Pedro Joaquín Chamorro was one of the strongest leaders of the bourgeois opposition to Somoza. He was killed by Somoza's men on January 10, 1978.

18.   Edmundo Jarquín is currently Nicaraguan ambassador to the U.S.

final shape. So, since then, especially during those years since
our triumph, I feel like those old usurers who live off the interest
of money lent out years ago. *Were You Frightened of the Blood?*
was first published in Caracas, then in Cuba, then in Nicaragua,
East Germany, Norway . . . an edition has just come out in
Spain, and this year there'll be one in Bulgaria and another in
Yugoslavia. It's a book that has begun to make its way around
the world on its own, and it's a book I finished almost ten years
ago. And that's really the last thing I've written. That's why I
say I feel like I'm living on my literary investments.

I look at literature with a great nostalgia, and I know if I had
it to do all over again I'd be a writer again. But one does not
choose in the abstract, but in the context of real conditions.
Such a luxury, for someone like me, is impossible in a country
like ours. Every day I feel that my commitment to my vocation
as writer is greater, but my commitment to my political work is
even greater . . . in the government, in the revolution. And I
don't see this situation changing, so that I could ask the Front to
relieve me of this responsibility and go back to being a writer.
That would be a dream. It's a possibility that doesn't even exist.

I try to keep my sensibility as a writer alive, like someone
keeping his pencils sharpened. I just use it in different ways.
And I try to be totally in touch with my political experience, my
contacts with different situations, people–which, in the last
analysis, is what the writer's raw material is. You might say I've
gone on to exercise my craft in another way. And I think my
political writing does have that literary ingredient which
shouldn't be lost. Now, Siglo XXI has put together some of my
political, ideological, and cultural writings of recent years, and
they will be published in Mexico in a book to be called *The
Golden Dawn.*

My head is always full of literary temptations, of projects . . .
novels and stories. I have a book of short stories planned, even
down to the title and the subject matter of some of the pieces. I
could easily write two or three more novels without having to
look for a new theme. That is to say, if by magic I could sit down
in front of a typewriter tomorrow, with ten hours a day guaran-
teed for work, I could begin to write again without any problem

at all. So I always feel like a writer on loan to the revolution. And I think that it's a much more serious road than that of the politician on loan to literature; they've never made very good writers.

The only act of pride I admit to is thinking myself a good writer, especially because I have so much respect for the craft. Because when I finished a book I did so with professional dedication; correcting, polishing, going back over it. I'm not a sloppy writer. In Latin America that should be the first condition, to really respect the craft, not to feel one can do without that. And I think that if I went back to writing tomorrow, I would still be the same writer with a respect for his craft, with respect for the blank page.

And Nicaragua is going to need good professional writers. Let's hope I can go back to being one of them. If not, well, at least I will have worked to prepare the ground so others can write. Helping the revolution move forward is the best way of guaranteeing that in the future there will be good writers, professional writers, here.

The revolution has created a culture that did not exist in the whole history of Nicaragua. And we see this in culture because it's a sensitive area that interests us, to begin with. Although, if you look at what the revolution has done in terms of building schools, the number of classrooms built, the number of children vaccinated, of rural health stations, people's stores, what you see is an enormous multiplication of the revolution's resources within our situation of limitations and of poverty. There's a centrifugal force here, the force of the people which is at the center of everything.

And this people's force is what makes our culture unlike any other in Central America. I feel we're at the stage of a cultural boiling point, as if there were all sorts of elements cooking at a constant high heat. What's going to come of all this? We don't know yet, because it's all still an unformed mass.

I wouldn't want to say that there's a novel of the revolution yet, a short story of the revolution, or a poetry of the revolution. But it's cooking there, at a high temperature, and I think some extraordinary things are going to come out of it. Here, there are going to be great poets, writers, playwrights, painters, sculptors, musicians, dancers, photographers, because that is the strength of the revolution, that it sets in motion that whole human mass and makes it possible for it to participate in tasks of which it never believed itself capable. And great creative individuals will come out of it.

It's just a matter of time. We aren't saying it can happen in four years. But we're going to have a new culture here, the foundations of which are being laid in the right way, with lots of creative freedom, without dogmatism, without sectarianism, encouraging freedom which is the very dynamic of the revolution. This is something that seems very important to me, that no one sits down to write recipes about what literature should be, what sculpture should be, what painting should be. Here we simply try to provide the possibilities for creativity.

That's the most important thing happening in Nicaragua. And in that respect there's absolute freedom, in form as well as in content. And it's something anyone can take part in. There's no cultural elite here anymore, just an enormous elite which is the entire people, who now share that possibility. And as long as we keep on preserving that line of free creativity, with the possibility for broad participation, good things have to come from it. If we had a good literature here when the country was elitist, what may we not expect with wide-open participation!

Vidaluz Menéses

We cannot talk about the revolution in the third person

Speaking of Nicaragua as "a land of lakes and volcanoes"[1] gives us in a few (though apt) words the image of a beautiful country in which a violent history lies always just below the surface. The same metaphors might apply to Vidaluz Menéses: woman, poet, Christian, an enthusiastic librarian, a mother for whom—paradoxically—the revolution has meant living apart from two of her children . . .

One must "begin at the beginning" in order to unearth—and to understand—the history of this woman: worker, poet, and revolutionary. That was precisely what I meant to do upon arriving at her home in the early afternoon of a warm day in May. Before sitting down to talk, I saw the house, the books, the paintings; I met her daughters, her aunt, and saw the lunch table set with a place for me. I felt at home in this house, so simple and full of natural hospitality. And we began a conversation, which will be somewhat edited and reordered here, but which I wish to offer with a minimum of cuts and changes.

1. Rubén Darío's words.

• *Vidaluz, let's talk first about your origins, your childhood and youth, about the things that may have left their mark on you as a woman, and as a poet.*

Vidaluz: After the revolution one realizes more than ever the need to define oneself, to identify oneself within a certain class. And that has led me to study something of how classes are divided in Latin America. My family, my development, belong to the middle class. I remember that among my first critical poems I made some which point out how "having" came to be an integral part of "being." My father was a member of Somoza's National Guard. And that has had extremely important repercussions in my life.

During my childhood and early youth my father was a lieutenant. We lived all over Nicaragua–the Guard was like that, always moving people around. I am the eldest of six brothers and sisters. A lieutenant's salary . . . well, it allowed us to live in a certain type of house, in a certain kind of neighborhood, and with a certain financial security. By the time I was older, just before I married, my father was a colonel; just after I married he finished his thirty years of service and retired as a general. Everyone in Nicaragua knows what happened in these cases: the higher the military rank–in the old society–the greater the economic possibilities and corresponding social level.

• *Your father's life, and also his death, have evidently marked your life in a crucial way; one senses this on reading your poem–perhaps one of the best known–"Last Postcard for My Father, General Menéses." Could you talk a little about your education, the origins of your calling as a poet, your Christian roots, and then speak at greater length about your father?*

Vidaluz: Okay. After undergoing the great trials of my life and coming to my total definition and option for the revolution, I've come to the conclusion that my feelings, in terms of the old regime, have more to do with sorrow than with hate. I have never been able to hate the enemy, but I feel a tremendous sorrow. Because someone I loved so much didn't share my ideals.

And that, I guess, is the central thread of my work. It's fundamental in the poem you refer to, thought to be one of my most
important. That poem deals with this balance. And yet I know
that with that poem I disappoint many friends, who have a right
to be disappointed because their own process, their own historic
commitment, was profoundly rooted in the liberation of our
people. Maybe the poem seems weak to them. I believe that
poetry has to be authentic, though.

   But going back to the beginning . . . what happened was that
my initial education in Christianity was with some old aunts of

mine, truly saintly women, typical of Nicaraguan small towns. They were primary schoolteachers in Matagalpa, very good and devout, much given to prayer. And they sowed in me my first religious concerns. At that time I had what you might call a magical sense of the Church—based on the ceremonies, the rites, the music, the incense. My first faith had as its basis that whole world which made a tremendous impression on me. Later my parents put me in La Asunción School, a school for upper-class girls. There I came in contact with a whole other dimension of religion, because the teachers had a higher cultural level.

• *Were you with Martha Cranshaw and that generation at La Asunción?*

Vidaluz: No, Martha came later. I was there with Michele Najlis. I was just going to mention Michele, as a matter of fact, because there you have a practical synthesis of religion, revolution, and poetry. Michele was very courageous, very intelligent, and I remember that the nuns were scandalized by her relationship with Fernando Gordillo. I remember the repercussions at school: "Michele is going to become a communist and stop believing in God."

I identified with what the *compañeros* were saying. I saw that a transformation of Nicaraguan society was necessary. But God was still a great source of conflict for me. A conflict that I didn't begin to resolve until after the Second Vatican Council. But we can't forget poetry either: for me it was all tied up together. When I was thirteen or fourteen years old—girls my age used to keep diaries—I really wanted to express what I was feeling. But instead of writing my diary in prose, I set out to express it in verse, with rhyme and all.

At that time I was reading Rubén Darío, a superficial Darío which was all that was available to us then. Also Amado Nervo and Gustavo Adolfo Bécquer. Later on, Carlos Pérez Alonso gave me a book by Neruda, *Twenty Love Poems and a Song of Despair*, and that book meant a lot to me. Later, I got my hands on a translation of North American [U.S.] literature by José Coronel Urtecho and Ernesto Cardenal; that's where I read

William Carlos Williams and Emily Dickinson for the first time. I began to write without using traditional meter then.

I remember that about halfway through high school Ernesto Cardenal showed up at La Asunción and asked for poems from those of us who were writing. I gave him mine. He selected some and took them to Pablo Antonio Cuadra, and so I was published for the first time. I think that must have been 1960 or '61. I published under a pseudonym, but it was a great stimulus. The synthesis of poetry, Christianity, and revolution began in those years; it's still with me today and has brought me a great inner peace. I'm strong enough now to define myself and overcome those last feelings of doubt . . . especially now that I have been able to really deal with my relationship with my father.

Perhaps I never went deep enough into revolutionary theory as such, and so never felt its full force. I always felt a conflict, an emotional one in the end. When I freed myself from that conflict, and became absolutely sure of my revolutionary choice, my poetry also became much clearer in reflecting that transformation, that conviction.

- *Vidaluz, I know it's still hard for you, but tell me about your father.*

Vidaluz: Well, you have to understand how I was drawn into the process of our country's liberation. Both my husband at that time and myself became close to the FSLN, collaborating in different ways, and there were moments in which my relationship with my father necessarily became tense. I must say there was a great respect on his part, but of course there were enormous silences as well. We never had violent confrontations; he never attacked me in front of others, or anything like that. But as it happened, on his retirement, Somoza named him ambassador to Guatemala.

By that time I was completely involved in the revolution. My husband and I began by getting safe houses for the comrades. You know, being married helped: my father, consistent with the ideas of that society, thought of my husband as being my "immediate superior," and if *he* allowed me to do such things then the best my father could do was to give him advice; once he told him to be careful. My father had the idea that I was an idealist, that I could be used by others because of my poetic and romantic nature . . . a father's natural concern. Being married gave me a certain leeway in that respect.

When I took part in the takeover of the United Nations building and got home with my clothes reeking of tear gas, there was no hiding it. My father didn't say anything, but my mother asked me to give him some sort of explanation. He was baffled by what I was doing. As I said, there was love and respect between us, but I was assuming an antagonistic position, and his reaction was logical, given who he was. I wrote two letters to my father. The first was in somewhat abstract language. I just felt the need to talk to him about our transformations as Christians. But the second was more decisive. I told him then that I was nothing more than the product of the education that they themselves had given me—by sending me to religious schools, by wanting me to have values such as justice and morality, and so forth. In my case, at least, those values were translated into another form. I had to be very clear in that letter, and I told him that I would always love him but that, unhappily, "I can't agree with you." I even said that history would condemn him but that I as his daughter would forgive him.

I'm going to forgive you—I told him—because you joined the Guard to have a career; you followed the footsteps of so many who were educated in it until they were for all intents and purposes contaminated with the privileges, and so on. But there can't be any justification for me, because I had the privilege of another kind of education. I felt that my moment in history was something else, my circumstances were different, and that greater demands were being made on me than on him. That's it, in synthesis.

• *Did he ever answer your letters?*

Vidaluz: No, never. We spoke once in a while, and once he even said that socialism might be a just option but that it would come through evolution. And we couldn't agree. Afterwards there was silence again. When Somoza named him ambassador to Guatemala, I told him not to accept–that it was a blessing that he had gotten out of the Guard, and he should dedicate himself to his own life and business then (he owned property), that he should get out of all that. But he always felt a commitment, that he had made a choice and had to stick to it. So he went as ambassador, and since there was a lot of international support for the Sandinista National Liberation Front, the Guerrilla Army of the Poor executed him on September 16, 1978.

• *He didn't die right away, did he?*

Vidaluz: No. They shot him on the sixteenth, and he died on the twenty-ninth. My sister and I went to be with him in Guatemala. It was a tremendous shock. I had already begun preparing myself for something like that, but still it was a terrible thing when it actually happened. I went to Guatemala and it seemed like some surrealist novel, because I was already completely committed to the liberation process, to the FSLN, and here I was traveling in a plane belonging to Somoza's air force, arriving at a hospital where my father was Somoza's representative and guarded by the security forces of Guatemala's repressive army . . . you can imagine what it was like!

My father had a bullet wound in the medulla, so he wouldn't have been able to walk, had he recovered. He would have been a quadriplegic. I prayed to God then that he would die; he would have been miserable the rest of his life. And for me, while he remained alive . . . [She weeps, pulls herself together, and goes on.] I remember speaking with a German doctor in charge of his case, and in the middle of the conversation I realized the man was a fascist. He was surprised when I said I wanted to know about my father's condition, and when I said that my father was also a victim of the Somoza regime. I could see that the man was shocked.

My family always saw me as the one with a higher cultural level or something, and later my mother had me speak to the press and give statements. When my father's condition deteriorated, I told one of the journalists that I hoped his blood would help bring peace to my country. An embassy functionary showed up then and said I should be careful about what I said because it could be utilized. I told him that as a Christian I stood behind what I had said.

My father died, and I returned to Nicaragua with my mother and the rest of the family. When I arrived, it was incredible: I got telegrams from Somoza people; one of them said, "We beg you to accept our condolences." And I got clandestine notes as well—from Ernesto Cardenal, for example, who sent me a beautiful letter comforting me and giving me support with his confidence in my commitment to the people. Alejandro Bravo, a brother poet, sent me a little piece of paper with the words, "I'm with you, Alejandro Bravo."

I also got a lot of support from my Christian group. That group has split as well, since the triumph of the revolution: some went with the people, and others stuck to that pseudo-Christianity which I consider one of the most comfortable positions in the abstract; a direct, vertical relationship with God.

• *Vidaluz, let's talk about poetry, your poetry. Did you publish a book before the revolution?*

Vidaluz: Yes, *La llama guardada [The Hidden Flame].* It came out in 1975. My husband financed it. I took the material to a printer, and they printed it. I tried to sell it in bookstores, but I ended up with whole crates of books; most of them I've donated now to the library system in the program where I work. The second book came out last year: it was a very beautiful and joyful occasion because it represents a start at achieving one of the goals of the Writers Union. Now one of the *compañeros,* who was published at the same time I was, says it's not just a matter of publishing; we have to promote the books and make sure they're sold.

• *Speaking of goals, why don't you talk some about the Ministry of Culture and the Sandinista Association of Cultural Workers; about the successes and problems you see in each institution?*

Vidaluz: That subject's been one of public discussion for several months now. Basically, I'm concerned that we manage to keep the criticism constructive. Criticism should serve the purpose of solving problems, and here we sometimes exaggerate the goals, as the young people today would say. For example, the Ministry of Culture has a profound importance for me. I'm a founding member, along with Cardenal and Daysi.

Just after the victory, I sent a note to the Ministers of Education and Culture. I myself made the mistake that we writers in the union are always bewailing, that of underestimating our condition as writers. I thought: What we have to do now is rebuild this country from the ruins it's in, and I chose my field because of its possibilities for service, in order to serve people. It's a technical field: library work. So I wrote and asked them to which of the ministries I should report for work.

The Ministry of Culture answered first. We had a meeting; I remember that Cardenal, Daysi, Carlos Alemán, and Ramiro Lacayo were there too. I arrived with Antonina Vivas, and there were some internationalists as well. We began to talk and ended up with a heap of flow charts on a blackboard. If there were deficiencies, they weren't intentional. No one knew how to go about creating a Ministry of Culture. The "conventions," for example . . . we didn't even know how to make them. It was like writing letters to Santa Claus . . . the victory was like a dream suddenly becoming real. One of us would say, Let's make a "convention" with such and such a country. Let's see, what do they make there? Let's ask them for a truck to go around collecting works of art which are a part of our cultural patrimony and are in the houses of the *somocistas* . . . things like that. We just had to learn as we went along.

I use a notebook a lot, and my assistant told me the other day: There's no time right now, but when things slow down a bit you should ask your secretary to organize and type up your notes because they'll be useful one day for reconstructing the history of the Ministry of Culture. And it's true. There are thousands of little things. I've often thought that the criticism the ministry receives is disproportionate. I always like to think, because I believe in people, that the nitpicking and preciosity of some *compañeros* is just a product of revolutionary enthusiasm. But I'd like them to be more realistic. Because sometimes they're so exacting that they make judgments which are destructive.

Regarding the Sandinista Association of Cultural Workers, I think the association has a very important role to play, and it's quite clear that its functions have yet to be clearly defined. The ministry is an institution, while the association is a guild. If we're clear about the definition of functions and objectives, we can see that they should be complementary. Precisely because of its institutional character, the ministry should be working intensively in all the arts; it should coordinate important events. The association should be able to respond to specific occasions, so as to free the ministry from that kind of pressure . . . so it can dedicate itself to a somewhat slower task, although it is one in which the association will also be involved.

• *Vidaluz, right now there's a lot of discussion about the question of writers as a group. Because the vast majority of Nicaraguan writers participated in one way or another in the defeat of the dictatorship, and the vast majority are with the revolution today. They work within the revolution, many in positions of great responsibility. But the Writers Union has had some problems consolidating itself. What do you attribute this to?*

Vidaluz: I can't be very categorical about that. The ASTC has had to give more attention to organizing other sectors, I guess; sectors where the artists weren't so solidly active within the revolution. In any case, the leadership of the Writers Union hasn't really been very functional; it hasn't worked well as a team.

We writers feel we are a part of the Nicaraguan people, a part of all the people, and we don't want to foster elitist positions, the idea that the writer should be some kind of privileged being. But we also have to recognize certain peculiarities or characteristics that artists as a group have. A writer has his or her own sensibility, his or her own way of moving, which can't be overlooked. You have to motivate people a bit to get them to join something like the Writers Union.

I'm not going to be simplistic and tell you the solution is just a change of leadership, but it would be a beginning. The union should have delegates, real representatives. I was even thinking it's pretty easy to criticize without committing oneself. Rosario [Murillo] pointed out the need for an executive secretary for the union. Because of my work priorities, I can't volunteer for that, but I'd be willing to work in a team with an executive secretary and other *compañeros* to try to achieve some cohesion in collective work.

• *Apropos of that, but backtracking a bit to more personal questions, what do you as a poet feel to be most urgent at this point in time? As far as your own work goes, what problems do you share with others which you feel need to be discussed here?*

Vidaluz: I've thought about this, of course, since it's exactly what we've been discussing in the Writers Union meetings. I think we cannot talk about the revolution in the third person. The revolution is the intimate commitment made by each one of us; we ourselves feel its urgency.

Yesterday, at the [Sandinista] Assembly, we talked about commitment. We have to organize brigades to go to the combat zones on the border. We have to postpone personal projects at this point. That's why we can't talk about the revolution in the third person—the revolution solving such and such a problem for *me,* guaranteeing *me* a space for my work. We all feel that need, but we see that it would be inappropriate to demand it in such a delicate and difficult moment. It continues to be a source of personal frustration that weighs on you, a limitation, but there are other, more pressing needs.

As the *compañeros* say, it's a commitment to future generations. All of us who have inherited a name in Nicaraguan literature in these early days of the revolution must bring new forms and content to the literature of the revolution. But that implies study, and exploration in your work, greater application. There isn't time, but it's not because they don't want to give you that time; it's because you're so struck yourself every day by the tremendous need there is on all sides, so much that has to be done, so many things that keep you from giving time to that other responsibility.

Someone said: So then we're going to be the sacrificed generation. And we must accept that. The generation after ours will begin to contribute in that sense. That's how I see it. But there's also something else; as limited as our work may be in terms of excellence, it is still more or less representative of Nicaraguan literature. And we have to publish and share all of this with so many among the people. We've got to go out and read—as we do—to the militia, to the sick, the elderly . . . and I feel that these experiences are very rich ones. Being able to share our poetry like that is to really democratize culture. So that's another dimension to the whole thing, something we can do with the time available to us.

You know, you discover things. One day Fernando Silva called and invited me to read with him at a club for diabetics. I imagined going to a hospital ward with all the patients swathed in sheets and with us reading to cheer them up or something. But we found ourselves in a hall used by people who aren't even hospitalized, but just need medical supervision. They have a health problem which is a daily burden, but which can be controlled with discipline and proper habits. They all arrived to celebrate the first anniversary of the diabetics club. The whole aim of the club is to work together to keep all the members following the diet and maintaining their controls. It was really beautiful.

• *Vidaluz, what are you writing now? Are you working on a new book of poems?*

Vidaluz: I've never written for a specific book. I write poetry because I need it, and all of a sudden I realize I have enough material for a book. I believe that a book comes as a result of the work you're doing over a period of time. As it happens, I have a few poems now, but I haven't published them and haven't been particularly interested in doing so. Because lately I haven't been able to work much on my poetry, I thought: Maybe it's better not to worry about publishing for a while. But at some point I will have to sit down and go through them and work on them more. Well, I'll show you what I have here.

To My Aunt Adelina

I watch you glide shadow-like
gentle presence inhabiting
our old home.
Beginning the day with your bath
in the chilly dawn,
the bells of Yalaguina
reverberating in our dreams.
The same ritual, still solemn
though no one awaits you now,
only your sister's letters
or the daily paper to be read on the sofa
immersing you artfully
in a world you barely touch.

It's strange, we've joined our solitudes
and I still remember you falling asleep
chin on your chest and hands in your lap
before finishing our bedtime story.
Now when our talk goes on and on
always revolving about a single theme,
because day after day you wonder
at the size and ages of my children
and you tell me, as if it just happened,
the story of your brother's death.
Let's sit and share this silence
or I'll explain the Sandinista Revolution,
the rectification of your teacher's pension
or our first year of victory,
why we women stand guard,
the militia uniform
and so many other new things you'll try to understand
before you have to leave them.

Lizandro Chávez Alfaro

The People's Sandinist Revolution opens up a space where we can look at life from new perspectives

In Managua the National Library can be found right in the middle of a large and teeming city market. That doesn't surprise anyone familiar with this revolution. Before the victory in 1979, the meager stock of books, in what might only by gross exaggeration have been called a library, was gathering mold in a locale by the lake; humidity, indifference, and abandon were the outstanding features of that place where people were supposed to go to seek the delights of reading. But, in any case, not that many people in Nicaragua knew how to read. What real importance could a national library have had in a country where more than half the inhabitants were illiterate, and potential readers lived under the daily repression of a dictator never himself known for his love of books?

Today Nicaragua's National Library is in a market. And in the afternoons—according to its director, the well-known novelist Lizandro Chávez Alfaro—the young people stand in line to get in. The modest facilities are hardly adequate for the needs of this population which, in 1980, learned to read and write. On entering the building, one is immediately struck by the eager groups of young people gathered around the tables, the orderly shelves of books, and the serenity that seems to emanate from all good reading rooms, even when they might easily be bigger or better

or fuller. I didn't go to the library to dwell on its virtues or limitations, but to find its director.

Lizandro is an affable man. He combines a certain air of the "gentleman" with an acute intelligence and a tendency to tease. As a novelist he stands out among the three or four good prose writers in the country; his novels have been serialized on radio and one of them has been adapted for television. He's expecting the interview and ushers me into his office, which is surprisingly Spartan. Through a single window behind him, a ray of morning light forms a sort of halo about his angular features. He doesn't wait for questions. He simply begins to speak about his life.

Lizandro: I was born in Bluefields in 1929. If the Atlantic
Coast seems remote or strange to us today, different from the
rest of Nicaragua, you can imagine what it was like then. Totally
cut off from the rest of the country. I began my studies at the
Moravian School, founded years ago by the Moravian mission
that came to Bluefields around 1843; all the kids just naturally
went to that school. The German missionaries came first, then
the North Americans around the time of the First World War.
And that's where subjection to foreign interests was most
crudely reflected.

Just imagine, at the Moravian School they taught us English,
and Spanish was thought of as a foreign language. I remember
studying almost everything in English. I have a very clear memory of Edelberto Torres[1] when he was working for the Ministry
of Education during the thirties and forties. He took a very
personal interest in trying to remedy that situation. I can almost
see him now, moving around Bluefields, coming to the Moravian School, making people uncomfortable because what we
wanted was to get them to teach in Spanish rather than in
English at that school.

I finished my primary schooling with the Moravians and
went on to the Christopher Columbus School in Bluefields for
my secondary education. And when I finally came to Managua,
it wasn't to continue school but to work. A brusque change. My
family was middle class; my father was a farmer and my mother
a housewife. Ours was a large family. My father had children
from a previous marriage as well as a number of children with
other women. I was the eldest of the four he had in his marriage
to my mother.

When I came to Managua it was to work in what was then
called the General Customs Collection Office; it was still ad-
ministered by the North Americans! My boss was one of those
gringos who had a commission in the National Guard; he was

1. Edelberto Torres, a Darío and Sandino scholar, a professor, and an
old-time Sandinista. Carlos Fonseca and others speak of him as "master."
Today, in his late eighties, he still writes, speaks, and teaches.

Colonel So-and-So. And that was another interesting experience for me, to be so close, so much a part of the dependent relationship that existed between Nicaragua and the United States, reflected even in something like our customs office.

• *What about literature, Lizandro? Were you already writing back then? How did you first become involved with the world of letters?*

Lizandro: Yes, I was writing then. But mostly I was drawing. I even had an exhibition of my drawings here in Managua. And I won a scholarship to Mexico to study painting. Oh, I had written some poems—like most Nicaraguans do—before leaving Nicaragua. But my main interest was painting then, and I went to Mexico to study at the San Carlos Academy, connected with the National University.

I went to Mexico in 1948. I was an adolescent. And of course in Mexico I read a lot more, and I had relationships with a number of literary people, poets and writers. And so, in spite of the fact that I had gone to study painting, I put my first book together. It turned out to be a single long poem, and you could already distinguish a tendency toward narrative. Although at that time the concept of "the early autobiography" wasn't so popular, that was more or less the intention of that first book-length poem. It's called *Hay una selva en mi voz [There Is a Jungle in My Voice]*. It was published in Mexico in 1950. So I continued studying painting at San Carlos, but by then I was definitely oriented towards literature as my life's work.

• *Who or what were the writers or books that had the most impact on you then?*

Lizandro: Hermann Hesse was very important to me. And of course I read a great deal of Latin American poetry: Carlos Pellicer, Octavio Paz, Efraín Huerta.[2]

• *You lived in Mexico for many years, didn't you?*

---

2. Mexican poets. Carlos Pellicer and Efraín Huerta, as well as being well known for their literary works, were identified with Left causes throughout their lives. They died only recently. Octavio Paz, also a well-known Mexican poet and essayist, has quite an opposite orientation.

Lizandro: Yes. For more than twenty years. I married there, a little late but I married. I lived in Jalapa, in the state of Veracruz, and for a long time I worked at the University of Veracruz. I was in charge of the radio station. Then I moved to Costa Rica, which was a way of getting closer to Nicaragua, and there I worked at the Consejo Superior Universitario Centroamericano [Central American University Council of Higher Education]. It was all a way of coming home.

• *When did you finally come home?*

Lizandro: July 19th, 1979.

• *Lizandro, during those last years leading up to the victory, did you have an active participation in the struggle in any way?*

Lizandro: Of course. Like all Nicaraguans living at that time in Costa Rica, and particularly in the context of the Central American University Council of Higher Education, where many of us were working, we lived more for Nicaragua than for Costa Rica. We collaborated in a great many tasks: research, propaganda, denouncing what the regime was doing.

• *Lizandro, you spoke a few minutes ago of your first book of poetry, with a narrative tendency. Which was your first real book of prose?*

Lizandro: *Los monos de San Telmo* [*The Monkeys of San Telmo*]. I finished it in 1960. But all books have their own biography, and it generally wanders for a while, acquires a history; sometimes there's a long wait before completion and publication. That book of short stories, *Los monos de San Telmo,* after searching all over for a publisher, finally found its way to the Casa de las Américas in 1963, and won the prize for short stories.

• *I think that was the first Casa prize won by a Nicaraguan, isn't that right?*

Lizandro: That's right. And the book has had a good life. It's been translated, partially or totally, into French, Italian, Polish, Hungarian, German.

• *Lizandro, why do you think a country like Nicaragua, which has such a wealth of poets, has so few prose writers?*

Lizandro: I don't think that's a Nicaraguan problem. It's something that's fairly generalized all over Latin America. And it seems to me it couldn't be otherwise. This continent is in a process of transition from the oral to the written tradition. So, in this process of transition, there are other genres which lend themselves much more easily to the creation of literature; such as the poem, or even the song. I think of the success of the new song movements in Latin America, for instance, and I believe they're successful at least partially because they're closer to the oral tradition. But narrative prose, the short story, and the novel even more, require a type of reader who is not yet exactly in the majority in Latin America.

• *Lizandro, tell me something about what you call the biography of your books.*

Lizandro: Well, with the cash prize I received from Casa de las Américas in 1963, I set out to write my first novel. That was *Trágame tierra* [*Swallow Me, Earth*]. I left Mexico City and went to live in a small port on the Gulf of Mexico. I had some friends there who offered me the use of a house, and that's where I wrote the first draft of *Swallow Me, Earth.* And it was three or four years before that book was published as well. I don't know if you've read it, but it's a very Nicaraguan novel. So much so that at one point in 1964 I was afraid that after so many years of being away I might be imagining a Nicaragua that had never really existed historically. And I came back here with that anxiety. And I found, sadly, that what I had tried to express in my book corresponded all too well to the reality of the country then: that sense of subjection, of dependence, exalted by one of the book's characters who is obsessed with the idea of building a canal through the country as the grand solution to all of its problems. And his conflict with the later generations, who know they must free themselves from that kind of dependence and correct the errors their parents committed.

The novel was finished in 1965, but it suffered a series of setbacks, and it was finally published by Joaquín Mortiz Press, in Mexico, in 1969. Then I began working on several themes. One is a theme which has always attracted me: the figure of

William Walker and the whole context in which he moved. I had an idea then for a novel, the provisional title of which was *Predestinado de ojos azules* [*The Chosen One with the Blue Eyes*]. But I wasn't really prepared then to take on a theme like that.

And I had another idea: the disintegration of a man exposed to that whole society of alienation, most dramatically felt in large cities like Mexico City. So I devoted myself to writing a novel called *Balsa de serpeintes* [*Serpent Raft*], which deals with precisely that. The myth of success created by the consumer society, where success itself becomes an invisible product. That novel also had to wait a while before it was published, and Joaquín Mortiz finally brought it out in 1976. By that time I had another book of short stories ready, *Thirteen Times Never*. It was published by EDUCA in Costa Rica the following year.

• *Have your books come out here in Nicaragua since the victory?*

Lizandro: Of course. The fifth edition of *The Monkeys of San Telmo* came out not long ago, and it's already out of print. And Editorial Nueva Nicaragua tells me they're planning on bringing out a new edition of *Swallow Me, Earth* this year [1983]; that will be the first time it will appear here in Nicaragua. I'm practically an unpublished author here, because my books could never get into the country in sufficient quantities for them to become known.

When *Swallow Me, Earth* came out in Mexico in 1967, bookstores here in Managua sent various orders to the press. And I remember Emanuel Carballo, at the publishing house, calling me in to his office one day to show me the packages that had been returned by the post office, with a seal on them here in Nicaragua which said they couldn't enter the country because of such-and-such an article of the Geneva Convention. We looked up the article; it referred to "subversive literature"!

• *Lizandro, when you returned on July 19th, 1979, the day of the victory, what vision did you have of what you might do—what role did you envision for a writer in a newborn revolution?*

Lizandro: Well, at first it was just a total euphoria. I arrived at the airport and all the Nicaraguans coming back sang the na-

tional anthem together. Even just hearing them announce the
fact that we were arriving at "Augusto César Sandino Airport"!
That alone told us we were coming to a completely new reality.
I remember I met a friend at the airport. We were wild with joy.
And she drove me into Managua. I was anxious to see what the
city looked like. Of course, we were coming in through the
eastern part of the capital; there were barracks of combatants
and columns of fighters still arriving.

So I was with this friend, and she didn't have papers for the
car she was driving. We were stoped by a young soldier. And
she told him: this is Lizandro Chávez Alfaro; he's come home,
and I have to take him to where some people are waiting for
him. And the young soldier said: "That's great, great that he can
come home! We sure have a lot to do here!" And that atmosphere of euphoria continued the following day, when tens of
thousands of Nicaraguans gathered in Revolution Square to
celebrate the victory.

I arrived and I was willing to assume any task that might be
assigned me. I was told to go and meet with the people who
were organizing the Ministry of Culture. We had a few of our
meetings at Government House, where everything seemed to
center then, and got together to talk about what a Ministry of
Culture might consist of. I presented a project for some television documentaries, and they sent me to INCINE, the new
film industry. So I worked at INCINE for several months right at
first.

One of the first things we did was a documentary on educa-
tion in the revolution. It meant a lot to me because it allowed
me to travel around the whole country, gathering material. I
was with INCINE until January of 1980, and then I went over to
Artistic Promotion—another part of the ministry—until 1981.
One of the things we were doing there was to organize the Ivan
Dixon Brigade with some of the artistic groups from the Atlantic
Coast. He got a whole show together, and presented it at the big
Rubén Darío People's Theater, here in Managua. And we
traveled with it to Havana as well, and to other parts of Cuba.
When I came back from that trip I took over the directorship of
the National Library. It was still over in Dambach then.

• *How many books were there at the old location?*

Lizandro: About sixteen thousand. We haven't been able to do another inventory since we've moved over here, but I imagine we must have somewhere in the neighborhood of thirty thousand volumes. Almost double what we started out with. This building, in the Eduardo Contreras Community Center here in the market, is not a definitive location, of course. But it's a step toward what we want for our library. When I took over, the first thing I had to do was to prepare the move, with some advisors provided by UNESCO.

• *Tell me something about the library today.*

Lizandro: There are days when we have close to eight hundred people come to the library. And we have an average use of six hundred. Those are numbers that strain our physical capacity to provide an adequate service. Especially in the evenings, which is when we have the most students coming in. In order for them to be able to study in minimally desirable conditions, they have to stand in line and wait for a seat to become available.

• *Lizandro, you took part in the creation of the Ministry of Culture, and you also participate in the work of the Sandinist Cultural Workers Association (ASTC). Could you speak about both institutions, their accomplishments and problems?*

Lizandro: Well, in the first place I want to say I think it was extremely astute of the leadership of the revolution to have appointed Ernesto Cardenal Minister of Culture. He's a man of tremendous worth, not only here in Nicaragua but also outside the country—as a priest, a poet, a revolutionary. He is just the right figure to be Minister of Culture.

Within our present possibilities, the present possibilities of the nation as a whole, and with the very scant resources which they've been able to assign the ministry, I think a great deal has been done. The promotion of crafts, for example, seems relevant to me—the status which crafts have acquired today as an authentic cultural expression; that's all ministry work. Another important thing the ministry has done has been the development of a film industry; something never before seen in our country.

Everything we do is part of the Sandinist People's Revolution as a whole, whether it's the promotion of a dance group, a film, a poetry reading, a crafts show, or an exhibit of paintings. And when it takes place outside the country, it reflects the efforts of all our people, a people engaged in a great historic task which is the making of a revolution.

As far as the problem of the writer goes, I've heard people say that to be a writer it's enough to be a revolutionary. And I've heard people say there's a necessary distance, a breach, between being a writer and being a revolutionary. I think both those positions are wrong. One first aspires to being a human being, and then a writer and a revolutionary . . . and it's all part of the same fabric. One can't separate those identities. How to do it—that's the main problem. I believe we can best achieve our multiple identity by taking on the tasks we are best fitted for.

I think we sometimes lose sight of the fact that we are no longer a revolutionary movement. We are a revolution in power. As a revolution in power, we must proceed with integrity, attending to all the nation's problems in an integral way. We must defend the revolution on all its fronts; on the military front, on the production front, on the creative front. All of that together goes into the transformation of society.

Of course, we're in an emergency situation at the moment. And many skilled workers, even inventors, must be mobilized to military tasks. That may be true of any worker, of someone in literature or in art as well as in any other area of activity. But our government would rather see each of us developing at what he or she knows how to do best.

As far as the ASTC goes, speaking for the Writers Union, it's clear that we lack organization. There are a great many reasons for that. I don't think we're going to get very far with sterile discussions about whether one is a revolutionary first or a writer first. We simply have to find the best way of functioning in our union.

But this isn't such a huge problem. There are other problems which seem to me to be much greater, more immediate, more important. Both the Ministry of Culture and the ASTC must define their areas of activity more clearly, and trace short-term, medium-range, and long-term goals. When that's done, the problems will work themselves out.

• *Lizandro, what are you working on now, in terms of your own writing?*

Lizandro: I am gathering together a series of essays, lectures, and articles I've done in the past three years. These basically fall into two categories: literature, and the history of the Atlantic Coast .

I think the People's Sandinist Revolution opens up a space where we can look at life from new perspectives. It's a new reality, which includes all of Nicaragua from 1979 to the present, and from 1979 back in time as well. Back in time, but from a different, a newer perspective–being able to speak of it with a freedom that did not exist before.

This revolution, like any revolution, wants to change reality. In order to change it, it must come to know it much more deeply, much more completely. And I think the craft of the writer can be very useful here, because we have a way of revealing aspects of reality that cannot be seen through other means.

Making literature, making prose or poetry in the revolution, isn't just a matter of looking at the topics, the characters, the events which have taken place since 1979. We must examine them in historical perspective. And I repeat, to the degree in which we can contribute to a greater knowledge of that reality, we will be contributing to the revolution. Because we will be enabling ourselves to know more about a reality that must be transformed.

Carlos Guadamuz

**There's so much, and if it's not
written down it'll be lost**

To interview Carlos Guadamuz is to speak with one of the few
survivors of those early years, those years when all the members
and collaborators of the Sandinista National Liberation Front
together weren't more than a few dozen men and women, and
that might be a generous count. To interview Carlos is, inevitably, to go back to the beginnings. And speaking with the poet
we speak, as well, with the fighter.

It's not hard to find Carlos at the "Voice of Nicaragua," the
state radio station he's managed since the 1979 victory. There,
in his simple office—dominated by a map of the world and
photographs of a few fallen brothers and sisters—he agrees to
the interview. He begins to speak without any prompting, but
he's talking about the station. From the beginning it's clear that
it's going to be hard to get him to talk about himself. His
memories tend to be plural, collective, and extensive. I ask him
to begin by telling me something about his youth.

Carlos: I don't know if you could really call us a generation,
but a group of us have known one another since adolescence;
we shared certain things, particularly our political concerns.
And we met sometimes, at school, in the neighborhood, or at
the demonstrations that took place then. We'd get together and

carry out incipient political tasks, even though they were pretty rudimentary at the time. The truth is, those of us who managed to stay alive till now are the same who twenty or twenty-two, twenty-three years ago were encouraged by the triumph of the Cuban Revolution and spoke, even then, of the triumph of a revolution in Nicaragua.

• *You grew up here in Managua?*

Carlos: Yes. I studied at the Baptist School, which was in the center of the city then, and also at the Pedagogical Institute—until they expelled me. I was also expelled from the "First of February"—now called "Rigoberto López Pérez"—so I have the honor of being the first student to have been expelled from that school (for political reasons; I wasn't a bad student). When I speak of those of us who managed to stay alive, I'm not only referring to human survival, but to political survival as well. Because many dropped out along the way, not necessarily betraying the cause but simply falling away, not having enough faith in an eventual victory.

• *Give me some names of those who were with you back then.*

Carlos: Well, there were Daniel and Humberto, the Ortega brothers. There was Jacinto Suárez, Lenin Cerna. And some who are dead now, like Selim Shible, Edmundo Pérez Flores, Casimiro Sotelo—who died in Monseñor Lezcano—and our glorious Julio Buitrago. Another survivor is Jorge Guerrero; he's a subcommander in the police. And Manuel Pérez who works in the Ministry of the Interior. The Roque brothers: Adrián and Rolando. It was a group that came together pretty much despite class differences, until we practically formed what people might call a "generation." The generation of Patriotic Nicaraguan Youth, of the CGT, and of the Socialist Party. But above all, Patriotic Nicaraguan Youth, which back then was the strongest organization; it could easily summon ten or fifteen thousand students for a rally. I'll never forget the great demonstration—it's really legendary—Patriotic Youth held on July 23rd, 1960, when we baptized Roosevelt Avenue "Sandino Avenue." I remember the sign that we put up was one of those

Coca-Cola signs; we removed the lettering, painted it red and black, and printed on it: "AUGUSTO CESAR SANDINO AVENUE." That was July 23rd, 1960.

• *One year after the massacre.*

Carlos: Exactly. In fact, it was to commemorate the massacre. The whole group I mentioned just now participated in that.

• *Carlos, were you already writing back then? Did you write poetry? What kind of contact with literature did you have?*

Carlos: Well, Fernando Gordillo was a big influence on us. By the time we had a more or less constant relationship with him, though, Fernando was already in a wheelchair. His physical disability kept him from playing an active role in the struggle by then. But even so, for us he was a political instructor; he taught

us the basics of revolutionary doctrine, and he also helped us
with our public speaking. Because, you know, Fernando
Gordillo was an excellent orator. And of course Fernando was a
poet, a poet and a member of the FSLN.

• *Carlos, what year did you join the FSLN?*

Carlos: In 1963.

• *Practically a founding member.*

Carlos: Yes. Because when we speak of the FSLN being
founded in 1961, it's not that the organization began playing an
important role in the country's political life that year. It came
out with a few proclamations by the end of 1962. And by then
Trinchera was already in circulation. And the first public action
that the organization carried out was the assault on the Bank of
America in March of 1963. I was recruited for the FSLN by
Lenin Cerna. It's not that I didn't have any political activity
before that; we had a loose group that was a kind of commando
unit. For example, we got arms or explosives any way we could,
and we tried to break into military installations and government
offices. We did some sabotage. And there were other groups like
ours, in other places, doing the same sort of thing, with the
same purpose: to take up arms against Somoza. But by 1963 we
all belonged to the FSLN, and that's when we met up with
Fernando Gordillo.

• *But it seems like you had more in common politically than literarily.*

Carlos: That's true. More than anything else, we were looking
for good speeches, proclamations for Guatemala Day, that sort
of thing. We wrote a few things of our own, too—the odd poem
or essay, but I don't think anything like that from those years
remains. And right here I should mention something that was
terrible, even back then: the reign of *La Prensa Literaria*. It acted
like a brake for those of us beginning to write back then.

• *It's interesting you should say that, because many writers I've
interviewed speak of* La Prensa Literaria *as the avenue for their first
publications. Could you explain why you say it was a brake?*

Carlos: *La Prensa Literaria* had the monopoly. *Novedades* made a couple of stabs at producing a literary supplement, but no one took it seriously. *La Prensa,* on the other hand, was taken seriously, and whether or not our poets—above all, those who published in it—want to recognize it, *La Prensa Literaria* was always markedly reactionary. Maybe Antonio Pablo Cuadra published a poem once in a while with a tinge of popular sentiment, but he as a person, and the supplement, were right wing.

We began to be clear about *La Prensa Literaria* because of a poet, a writer who was a little bit crazy, named Idelfonso Solorzano. We called him Ildo Sol. He knew something about scientific socialism, and he wrote. And he was a relentless enemy of Pablo Antonio's. He was the first to understand Pablo Antonio's real attitude toward us. We were young guys; seventeen, eighteen years old at the time. And Ildo Sol helped us perceive what that whole thing was about. Pablo Antonio might publish a halfway positive poem once in a while, but his true function was to maintain a whole structure of right-wing literary activity.

We felt the rejection from the moment we'd arrive at *La Prensa Literaria* and say, "Look, Pablo, here are some poems," and the man would simply say no. Like the time he even went so far as to reject writings by Ricardo Morales Aviles (one of the greatest intellectuals our country has produced); he literally threw Ricardo's work at Doris, now Commander Doris Tijerino, who was an activist in the FSLN at that time. He told her: "This is no good. I can't publish this stuff." Poems Ricardo had written in prison.

So we wrote poems and they remained unpublished. We were the only ones who read them. And we despaired of ever seeing them in print, because we weren't going to get down on our knees with Pablo Antonio. We weren't going to beg him to publish us.

• *When I first heard your name, Carlos, many years ago, it was the name of a combatant, but it was also the name of a poet. And I had seen your poems.*

Carlos: Well, by the time you saw my poems, the CUUN [University of Nicaragua Student Center] had begun publishing *Taller.* That was our great alternative, the place where we revolutionaries could publish our verse. We began publishing when we were in prison; that's where we really began developing as poets. Because there wasn't much else to do there.

- *Tell me about your life as a poet in prison.*

Carlos: Our creativity in prison had certain charactéristics. For one thing, it was a collective effort. When any one of us wrote a poem—Julián Roque wrote a lot, I remember—each poem, each line was furiously gone over by all the rest of us. Sometimes we discussed a single poem for hours on end. And the finished product might be 40 percent by the guy who wrote it, and 60 percent by the rest of the *compañeros.*

- *What year were you taken prisoner?*

Carlos: In 1969.

- *Until . . . ?*

Carlos: Until December of 1974. The 30th of December. I was in prison for five years and five months.

- *And who was there with you?*

Carlos: Jacinto, Daniel, José Benito Escobar, Lenin Cerna, Oscar Benavides, Julián Roque, Leopoldo Rivas, Manuel Rivas Vallecillo, and Francisco Ramírez. But Francisco was freed in 1973. If we were to judge our work on its literary value, really the only work that stood out there was Daniel's and mine. But in evaluating the importance of those years, we have to look at the work in terms of the impact it had on our grassroots-level members, the membership base of the organization. Our base membership, and even the students, had read very little because of the difficult conditions that existed in the country at the time. So what we wrote played an important role; politically speaking, it played a formative role among students and our base-level membership. We didn't necessarily intend for it to be that way, but that's the way it was.

• *How was your work distributed among all these people?*

Carlos: Well, we'd send our writings out with our relatives, or with a sympathetic guard. That way they'd get to our comrades of the FSLN, especially Ricardo, and he processed much of what we wrote. And when he thought it was worthwhile, he'd have it published. In the case of my book,[1] that was even earlier, and it was Camilo[2] who was in charge of publishing it. Daniel also wrote a book in prison, but the manuscript was later lost when Somoza's security forces searched a house where it was. It was lost forever, unfortunately. It was a book Daniel wrote on the origins of class struggle during the colonial period.

• *Carlos, I imagine you had a lot of time to read during those years in prison. What books interested you in those days?*

Carlos: Well, we had to read in secret, but we did read. Steinbeck's *Grapes of Wrath* was a book that impressed us a great deal. The Russian writers: Dostoyevsky. And all the Latin Americans: García Márquez, Cortázar.

• *Carlos, tell me something about the history of* And the Houses Filled Up with Smoke. *I know you wrote it in 1970, at the so-called Model Prison, at Tipitapa. But tell me about it.*

Carlos: The book was an attempt to recreate the figure of Julio Buitrago from bits of his conversation, things I remembered. It might seem to people today too personalized to write a book about a single member of the FSLN, but the impact Julio had on all of us in the organization was something difficult to describe. The way he died, it hit all of us . . . hard. There wasn't a single one of us who wasn't moved, who didn't feel his courage in our own flesh. It was the first combat of that kind in the country.[3]

1. *Y las casas se llenaron de humo* [*And the Houses Filled Up with Smoke*], published after the victory by Editorial Nueva Nicaragua, Managua, 1982.

2. Camilo Ortega Saavedra, Daniel and Humberto's brother, killed in the Monimbó uprising in February of 1978.

3. On July 15, 1969, the house where Julio Buitrago and Doris Tijerino were working was surrounded by members of the National Guard, and Doris was captured. Julio held out against hundreds of guardsmen until they finally killed him. His resistance was truly heroic.

• *I don't think the impact was only on members of the FSLN. The dictatorship made the mistake of showing that combat on TV, and it made a tremendous impression on the entire population, on everyone who saw it.*

Carlos: Yes, the impact was generalized. Because it was the first time in Nicaragua that there was such a brutal one-sided attack, with a tank and everything, against a single house. But you can imagine, if the impact on the general public was great, what it must have been like for us. So I began working on the book, and Daniel and Jacinto read it over. We decided to smuggle it out, and the comrades on the outside said yes, it was worth publishing. And so it became study material for *compañeros* working underground and in the FER [University Student Revolutionary Front].

A source of pride for me, about this book, is that Commander Omar Cabezas told me that one of his last tasks before going underground was, in fact, to mimeograph, collate, edit, and distribute my book. It was very well received by the student population there in León. One of our *compañeros* who died in Jinotepe, in 1973 or '74, had the book among the literature found on him. I couldn't have imagined that the book would be so useful in terms of educating our rank-and-file members, but that happened because there was a real need of material not only on scientific doctrine or the experiences from other countries, but work which was our own as well, about our own revolutionary experiences.

One thing people have told me was important in that respect was the attention given to the role of women. There were two women comrades who played a very important role in our underground movement, and they are spoken of in the book. According to some of our *compañeros* on the outside at that time, that proved important for the women university students in León, to see the presence of those *compañeras* underground playing a role as important as that of any man. Daniel himself highlights that in the introduction he wrote for the book: the participation of women.

• *After the victory a commercial edition of the book has come out. When was that?*

Carlos: On the third anniversary of the triumph, last year [1982].

• *And what sort of reception has it had? Above all, how do you feel about the book today?*

Carlos: The new publication has been very moving for me. Because all those things we did so long ago, they bring back memories, you know . . . life in prison, for example. And Lenin Cerna's drawings in the book. It wasn't just because someone thought he should illustrate the new edition; there's a reason for it. In prison Lenin was always painting. He did portraits of us all, he did landscapes, all sorts of things which we smuggled out in order to get a pound of meat or something from our collaborators. Because in those days collaborations were scant. I always like to tell the story about the time when the Front was so poor that, according to Lenin, Carlos Fonseca came home all smiles one day and said, "Goddam, we got a great contribution!" "Wow, what did you get?" "A subscription to *La Prensa!*" The paper was worth thirty cents then; the subscription was nine *córdobas!* That'll give you an idea of the poverty we lived in at that time.

So Lenin would paint and he'd say, "Well, I'll make some Christmas cards." He'd do the drawing, and one of us would write a verse or an inscription of some kind. Then we'd all sign it and send it to people we thought might be able to collaborate with us. Some responded by sending a pound of coffee, or a meal ordered from a restaurant. Things like that. That's why I say Lenin's drawings aren't in the new edition just for decoration. They are part of that whole tragedy of struggle, because a struggle carried out under those conditions, apart from being heroic, is tragic.

• *Carlos, what about now, since the triumph? How did you get into radio? Did you have any previous experience in the medium?*

Carlos: Well, before going underground I worked a while as a journalist for radio. You know how things are in the revolution. If you were a secretary in a bank, for example, after the triumph you might have to be the manager. We've had to improvise. We've had no choice.

• *Have you been able to keep writing during these years after the victory?*

Carlos: I haven't put my mind to it. Maybe if I did, I could do something. My friends are constantly telling me I should, asking when I plan on starting to write again. Some *compañeros* have practically told me it's my duty to the party, that I must record a whole series of important experiences. Because out of that whole generation, the whole group, I guess I'm one of the ones with the most time. Daniel can't do it; Tomás can't; Jaime can't; Leopoldo, Lenin.[4] I'm not under nearly as much pressure as they are. Comandante Núñez[5] himself is constantly insisting that I start writing again, because I know so many things firsthand, having been a part of that heroic time. I personally witnessed so much, with Carlos, with Silvio, with Danilo Rosales, Selim Shible, Germán Pomares.[6] There's so much, and if it's not written down it'll be lost.

• *Perhaps this takes us to a final question, about the writer or the creative person in a revolutionary process. It's something which has stimulated a great deal of discussion here lately. Would you like to say something about that?*

Carlos: Well, Margaret, I know that in the last few weeks there's been a sort of polemical discussion, especially within the Writers Union, about the role of the writer in the revolution. Some have even gone so far as to pose the famous (stupid) question: Which comes first, the writer or the revolutionary? Something like the old chicken-and-the-egg problem. When all is said and done, discussions like these are always positive because many different opinions are expressed. But it seems to me that in this case the discussion arises out of an atmosphere of some confusion. I was amazed, frankly, that in a room full of writers, most of whom have a long experience—a number of

4. Daniel Ortega, Tomás Borge, and Jaime Wheelock are members of the FSLN's National Directorate. Leopoldo Rivas is a commander in the army, and Lenin Cerna is head of National Security.

5. Commander Carlos Núñez, member of the National Directorate of the FSLN.

6. Comrades who fell in battle at various times during the struggle.

years involved in this business of Nicaraguan literature–they'd be asking all these redundant questions. These questions were answered a long time ago here in Nicaragua. In the sixties, in the seventies, when the same questions came up, the same polemics, the same discussions–with one difference. Then the answer was clear for everyone: make the revolution.

A writer can't be apolitical. Nobody is apolitical in this world. And that's why I say that those questions are outmoded now, historically speaking. We've gone beyond them. Above all, the men and women who were present at that meeting of the Writers Union. Because, well, if it's a question of young people who are just starting out, who are just emerging from the workshops and taking their first steps, then logically they have the right to pose that kind of a question for themselves: "Now that I'm a writer, what is my role in the revolution?" But among those of us who have been writing for a long time here, with the kind of experience we Nicaraguans have–as protagonists or even as witnesses of our revolutionary struggle–well, the question seemed a little inappropriate to me.

It's as if a combatant of the EPS [People's Sandinist Army] were to ask himself or herself, "Well now, what is my role in the revolution?" Because, especially right now, the revolution is in a life-or-death situation. First, we have to win this current and decisive battle, perhaps the last battle against imperialism, the last in the sense that it's going to be the definitive one, because if we win this one imperialism will have to face the fact that for this revolution there's no turning back. At this point in time, then, it's imperative to put all our resources toward that principal objective which is the consolidation of the revolution. Later there will be a time and a place to talk about other things.

I remember in one of the congresses of Cuban writers, one of the congresses of their Writers Union, in 1978 or thereabouts, if I'm not mistaken, Armando Hart[7] referred to this famous polemic (because it doesn't come up only in Nicaragua but in all countries with experiences similar to our own, that is, which

---

7. Armando Hart, member of the Politburo of the Cuban Communist Party, is Cuba's Minister of Culture.

have a revolution in power). He said that when José Martí[8] was fighting, many of the writers and poets of his time asked him: "Maestro, why do you, a great writer, a great hope for world literature, not dedicate yourself to literature? You have a greater future as a writer than as a soldier." And Martí responded: "Now we have to fight a war. When we've won it, there'll be time for literature."

So, Hart said, we struggled, and we made the revolution. And we struggled to consolidate it. We won the war; now let's make culture, he said. I'm talking about a recent speech by Hart, almost twenty years after the triumph of the Cuban Revolution. Even at that point in time the old controversy was still alive in Cuba, and Hart felt compelled to address it at that congress. So what did Hart teach us, what did Martí teach us, what did our most important intellectuals teach us—Leonel Rugama, Ricardo Morales? That we are still at war. Of course, we're not going to throw all literary and intellectual creation away because of that. But at this point in time the most important thing is to defend, to consolidate the revolution. Because in order to think, in order to write, first you have to eat. First you have to live.

8.   José Martí, one of the great modernist poets of the Spanish language, as well as author of many volumes of essays, articles, fiction, plays, and criticism, was a central organizer in Cuba's War of Independence. He died in battle in 1895.

Beltrán Morales

I heard the trees were innocent

Beltrán was waiting for me when I drove up in front of his house. He was rocking in one of those old wicker rockers typical of Nicaraguan colonial cities, and as I got out of the car and walked over to him I thought how much he *looks* like a poet, how much he's always looked like a poet, from the time I first met him in Mexico City almost twenty years ago. Now in his late thirties, his mental illness has finally been diagnosed and he can pretty much deal with it. I knew that he had just emerged from a recent bout with his problem; I noted a slight tremor in his hands, and he was wearing dark glasses. But the poet was there, intact. Beltrán is a poet who knows where his star is, and just goes on following it.

The evening was lovely and the street peacefully quiet. We could have begun the interview right there, on the porch, but I wanted to talk where Beltrán works. So we went inside and settled in his tiny studio, surrounded by books, papers, the very small table that serves as his desk, the old typewriter. I wanted to listen to what the poet would say, as close as possible to the cardboard box filling with pages and pages—more than eight hundred at this point—of his novel in progress. So we made ourselves comfortable and began. Beltrán speaks rapidly—the words literally tumbled from his mouth.

Beltrán: My class origin is simple: I belong to that very broad, very urban, very San Sebastián middle class. I'm talking about San Sebastián, the neighborhood where I grew up. I began to write at the age of fourteen. I was in my third year of high school then, and filled a notebook with verses I called *Triangles and Poems,* which of course I've lost. But I published my first poem in *Ventana,* the magazine Sergio Ramírez and Fernando Gordillo edited. Or maybe that's not true. Maybe my first poem was published in *La Prensa Literaria,* founded by Pablo Antonio Cuadra.

In any case, they were three or four short poems. I can't remember who it was who said recently that there really are no long poems, just a succession of short ones linked together. I think it was Pablo Antonio who published that series of three or four of my poems, influenced by García Lorca; they were called "Three or four poems for a white girl who saw herself as green." They were about a neighbor of mine who had green eyes, just like in the song.

My family was originally from Contales, but they moved to Managua when my father was two years old. We lived in an enormous house in San Sebastían. There were five brothers in all, and some nine cousins, a large family. And everyone in our family, everyone in the whole neighborhood, was influenced by the Christian Brothers, at the LaSalle. It's not true, what a conservative writer once said, that the Central American School was for the upper classes, the Pedagogical Institute for the middle classes, and that the workers' children went to the Salesian. Because the truth is there were kids from all classes in all the schools.

• *Beltrán, I remember we first met years ago, in Mexico. In the sixties. Why did you go to Mexico?*

Beltrán: By then I was already beginning to suffer from this illness of mine; it's a manic-depressive psychosis. But no one understood that kind of illness much in those days. I'd had the first symptoms in 1967, when I was twenty-two. I was at Solentiname, then, for about three months, visiting Ernesto Cardenal. Ernesto had just come back from Mexico and he had contacts with the old Benedictine monastery at Cuernavaca; it had been converted into a psychoanalytic center and he suggested that it might be helpful for me to go there. So I did. I remember I had two gold Parker pens in my pocket.

There, in that center, I met a man about fifty years old with a moustache. He looked like García Márquez. I always tell people it was García Márquez. No one can take that idea from me. Of course I knew it wasn't; just someone who looked like García Márquez. So that was 1967, and one day a man dressed in a 1940 suit with wide lapels arrived. It was the poet Cardenal, who had come back to visit. I wanted to leave Cuernavaca; I was never happy there. So the poet told me to go back to Nicaragua, to go home. And I did.

• *And your first book?*

Beltrán: *Some Sun,* it's called. Sergio Ramírez helped me get it published. It came out from the University of San Carlos Press, in Guatemala. That was in 1969; I was already twenty-four. Someone once asked me if the title was influenced by Octavio Paz's *Eagle or Sun,* but it isn't. And it's not from a verse by Jorge Guillén either, that great Spanish poet, one of the greatest in the language. *Some Sun.* There are political poems in that book; for example, one which asks "what did you do . . ." based on a verse from Neruda's *Canto General.* Another is called "Mary's Children." I'm really not a very political poet. I think those poems have lost their authority. They're nothing but memory now, a testimony of the times. That's why I think it's a risky business writing political poetry. Because it tends to fade like that. Nothing more than a memory. A photograph in an album. I was already repeating the Sandinista slogan back then: *Patria Libre o Morir* [Free Homeland or Death], the same as you hear on everyone's lips today. But there were very few of us who dared utter that slogan back then. So you see . . .

• *Beltrán, how did you begin writing poetry? How and when?*

Beltrán: I don't remember. I know there was a *malinche* tree in the schoolyard. That tree must have been about a hundred years old. And when we misbehaved they punished us by making us stand under it. That old *malinche.* But one day they cut it down. The schoolyard looked empty without it. And I wrote a poem to its absence. Of course I can't find that poem either. Brother Emiliano must have kept it. He was a strange man; "dead face," we called him. He taught Spanish literature. I think that's when I began writing seriously, with dedication.

• *When did you come back from Mexico?*

Beltrán: In 1967, if I remember correctly. But in 1970 I went to Costa Rica. And then I came back again in 1973. And now I'm here to stay. In 1975 I published *Without Yellow Pages,* a collection of my articles published over ten or twelve years. Literary criticism mostly. I think it's a pretty good book; oh, it's got its defects, but it has some saving graces as well.

• *What other writers have influenced you, Beltrán?*

Beltrán: Well, that has a lot to do with my illness, with my manic-depressive psychosis. Cycles of depression and cycles of mania. In my manic phases—I'll never forget one of them, in 1973, I discovered Lezama Lima. I read Goytisolo's edition, published in Barcelona. And I also discovered Jorge Guillén. For me they are the best in the language. I've never felt so passionately about any other author. There are writers like Nabokov I've tried to read, but I can't. I don't like Nabokov because all his characters play tennis. They have nothing to say to me.

When I discovered Jorge Guillén's poetry, I did a kind of survey among my friends. I wanted to find out what they thought of him. And they all said almost the same thing, that he was too hermetic, an author who requires discipline to be able to read him. I've always maintained that prose allows speed but poetry demands that you take your time with it. Those are my two key authors, you might say.

• *Beltrán, what did the victory of the revolution mean for you, for your poetry and for your life?*

Beltrán: The victory was incredible. Everyone said, it's like a dream come true. And even now it seems too good to be true.

• *Were you here when it happened?*

Beltrán: Yes, I was here on July 19th. I went to the Plaza with Rolando Steiner, and there was this huge mass of people, cohesive, enthusiastic; it was marvelous. I'm going to say something you might not like, in fact it might bother a lot of people, but it's true. For me—in my personal case—the revolution meant the end of opposition. There's no longer any way of being an opponent. One went from being an opponent to a completely opposite position, being on the side of the revolutionary government. As if all those years of struggle had ended . . . know what I mean?

Of course, it's only my point of view. Because it's true, like the saying goes, "Sandino lives, the struggle goes on." The struggle goes on, even if you're not in the mountains anymore. And so I do feel that in one way or another I'm contributing to the struggle, participating in the cultural brigades, even though I'm not carrying a rifle.

• *Beltrán, how do you see the cultural process within the sociopolitical process of the revolution? How do you see the creative process here? Yours, and everyone else's? Although perhaps there are two different answers . . .*

Beltrán: Well, I think one must measure the cultural aspect of a revolution by its literary and cultural movements. We have the Sandinista Cultural Workers Association. It's something we can all take part in, and we all feel united in some sense. We all feel like brothers and sisters.

Then we have the poetry workshops. I've been giving them a lot of thought, mulling them over in my head. And there's something there that bothers me. All the voices are the same. They're all the same. Too much uniformity. It's impossible to tell one would-be poet from another, in those workshops.

• *And why do you think that is?*

Beltrán: Frankly, I don't know.

• *Beltrán, has the revolution changed your own creative process in some way?*

Beltrán: Yes. I'm writing this novel. Since 1978, when I wrote my long poem, "International Bread," I haven't written any new poetry. I've devoted myself exclusively to my novel. Maybe I'm not really a poet anymore. Or . . . I don't know what's happened to me. Maybe I haven't found my personal voice yet. At this late date—I'm thirty-seven years old—I have the impression that my voice is an echo, my poetry is an echo.

• *And the novel?*

Beltrán: To begin with, it's called *The Box Factory.* I use the term "box" as a synonym for commonplace, for ordinary. In Nicaragua, people used to say "it comes right out of a box," meaning something is commonplace, that it's a cliché. The expression isn't used much anymore. I call my novel that precisely because it tries to *avoid* the commonplace. At the same time, it cannot help but fall into the commonplace, into the cliché, because the whole language is filled with them. In the novel I say that the box is the tongue's soul. And we couldn't live without clichés, it's true. The protagonist's name is Cell.

• *Are you the protagonist?*

Beltrán: Of course. The protagonist, Nathan Cell, is me. It's a novel about friendship; and more than friendship, it's about friends. I try to find an equivalence table of surnames, and another of names. For example, I had thought that all the Carloses could be called Emeritos, and all the Ernestos Pastor. It's really a problem, because there are so many Carloses, so many Ernestos, Ramiros, Franklins. There are too many people in the novel. I've created a monster. It's already too long, eight hundred pages, single-spaced. I don't really know what I'm going to do. Maybe publish several volumes . . .

I have the example of my father. My father is a very important character in the novel. His name is Kiko Cell. He writes novels in French, on wrapping paper. He writes them in French and then he translates them into Spanish. He has a closet full of novels; they're probably pretty bad, but what matters is the character, how he evolves. He has that daily discipline, because every day he sits down for at least three hours and writes. That's really true about my father; it's authentic.

• *How does your illness affect your creativity, Beltrán?*

Beltrán: When I'm in my manic phase I read a lot. I devour books, one after another, passionately. When I'm depressed, I generally just feel like sleeping and sleeping and sleeping. Total inactivity. When I'm in-between I can sit down at the typewriter, correct my things, write new things.

• *Are these phases long or short?*

Beltrán: There's no specific length of time. It can be a month, two, three. When the manic state is very pronounced, I have to be hospitalized. Once when I was in the hospital I heard the trees were innocent.

• *So you've learned to live with it?*

Beltrán: Sure, I've learned to control it. When I feel overly excited, I go to the doctor and he changes my treatment, increases the sedatives. I think my illness is something like alcoholism.

• *Beltrán, what do you think of the meetings being held these days at the Cultural Workers Association? About the discussions concerning creativity and revolution . . .*

Beltrán: The ones doing the most talking are those who went to the Asunción . . .

• *Those who went to the Asunción?*

Beltrán: Yes. Vidaluz, Gioconda, Michele . . . It's just as well that Rosario Murillo went to the Teresiano,[1] and not to the Asunción . . .

• *And the writers' problems?*

Beltrán: Well, all this about people not having time to write these days; it's a very delicate question, really, isn't it? Personally, I can't complain because the revolution has been very generous to me. First, because I was always a collaborator of the FSLN. I worked with Carlos Fonseca, with Ricardo Morales.[2] And second, because I'm ill. So they've given me a stipend, modest but enough to live on. I get by, and I can devote myself to writing. But in the case of many of the others, I can understand that it's a difficult question. Although I think they exaggerate, too. It's always possible to find one or two hours a day to write. You don't hear Ernesto Cardenal complaining that he has no time to write, now do you? I've never heard him complain anyway. He keeps on publishing his poems. And new ones. Every day he publishes a new poem. In his most recent poem,

1. The Asunción and Teresiano were the two Catholic schools for upper-class girls in Managua.
2. Carlos Fonseca was the founder of the FSLN, and Ricardo Morales was a member of one of the organization's first National Directorates. Fonseca was killed November 8, 1976; Morales September 18, 1973.

Ernesto Cardenal tells us that his grandmother had a gardener. It's useful to have a piece of information like that. Right there in the pages of a magazine. Proof of it!

• *Beltrán, you'll be going north soon in one of the cultural brigades. What kind of an experience do you expect that to be, sharing with the soldiers on the front lines?*

Beltrán: I just hope to communicate with my brothers and sisters who are fighting, and find some kind of direction myself in that contact. And maybe I'll even be able to write a poem or an article or something, to share what I've experienced, so others will be able to have it too.

Ernesto Cardenal

My whole life has been a path
leading me to the revolution

Ernesto Cardenal has become a legend in his lifetime. More important, he has been a prophet in his land: the first Nicaraguan priest to join, in the late sixties, the Sandinista National Liberation Front (FSLN).

The second son of a wealthy family in the conservative city of Granada, he took part in an attempt in 1954 to overthrow Somoza García. As a poet, he was more deeply influenced by Ezra Pound than by his native Darío, and his verse is both profoundly Nicaraguan and intensely visionary, even in its details.

A man in need of the flesh as well as the spirit, he nonetheless responded to a clear call to the religious life; and learned from the Trappists in Kentucky, the Benedictines in Mexico, and a traditionalist seminary in Colombia before founding his contemplative community which thrived between 1966 and 1977 on a remote island in Lake Nicaragua.

Today Ernesto wants nothing so much as to return to that island—Solentiname—and write the wonders of this revolution, its tenderness and pain. But the revolution needs him as its Minister of Culture, and he has considered himself a committed militant in the Sandinista vanguard since the day, in 1976, when he agreed to accept the mission of going to the Bertrand Russell Tribunal in Rome, in order to denounce the terror and crimes being wrought against his country's peasant population by the son of the man he had tried to overthrow twenty-two years before. He is a member of the FSLN's highest body, its Sandinista Assembly.

Ernesto has said, on more than one occasion, "I now see that my entire life, my initial commitment to God, my time with Merton in Kentucky, the years at Solentiname, the poetry, everything, was part of a single road to the revolution." And so he will stave off a bit longer his need for solitude and time to write, while the revolution needs him to harvest poetry and painting workshops, theater groups, crafts collectives, musicians, and dancers across this wounded and creative land.

And when Ernesto says his life has moved along a single road toward revolution, he means as well a single road toward God. God and the revolution are quite tangible in his concept of the world, and they are almost indistinguishable in the way he has chosen to live his dream. His has been a life of service, but service as the poem is service: brilliant, luminescent, visionary, of the spirit . . . never forgetting that the body is, or should be, one with the spirit.

Since the Solentiname days, this poet-priest has chosen his manner of dress, and it has rarely varied: ordinary blue jeans; the white *cotona,* or simple loose-fitting shirt, common to the Nicaraguan peasant; and a black beret. In this same attire, and weather permitting, he has spoken before crowds of thousands— or tens of thousands—in countries throughout the world, received international awards and honorary doctorates at the most prestigious universities, and gone hunting for fishing bait on his beloved island. Once I have seen him in militia uniform, back in 1981, when the first of the recent round of U.S. military maneuvers threatened Nicaragua, and members of the FSLN donned the brown shirt and olive green pants as a sign of protest and readiness.

I have known Ernesto Cardenal since 1962, when—with other poets in Mexico City at that time—our basic concern was the sharing of the poem: from North to South, from South to North. I was just initiating an eight-year experience with a bilingual poetry journal, *El Corno Emplumado.* Ernesto had just

come from his time with Thomas Merton at Gethsemani. Colombia, Solentiname, and the victorious Nicaraguan Revolution were all still ahead of him.

The interview, then, was important to me not only in the context of this book, but in the context of a life. A life that has been meaningful to my own as it has been to his people and their historic decision of struggle. As accessible as the man is—almost anyone dropping by his office in what used to be the mansion occupied by Somoza's wife, and which today houses flutes and marimbas, painted birds and indigenous sculpture, may climb the short flight of stairs to the second-floor loft—the demands of the revolution have meant almost constant travel for him.

If *el padre*[1] is in the country, and not besieged by matters of state, he will stop and listen, ask questions of the visitor, and share his experience of this country where "we can offer ad-

1. the Father.

visors to any army in the world . . . in matters of poetry!" If, on
the other hand, he is out of the country, you might have to wait
for him to return from Washington or Frankfurt, Buenos Aires
or Madrid, before there's a chance for conversation. In this
particular case, we had to wait for my return from Canada and
his from Los Angeles before sitting down to talk about the
poems he would much rather be writing.

It finally happened, though. In his simple office, after some
initial talk, we began with the usual: childhood influences, the
first encounter with the poem.

Ernesto: I wouldn't say Darío influenced me, not really. But
Darío evoked the poem in me. Discovered the poet in me,
perhaps. Even before I learned to read. I remember when I was
very small, my father—who wasn't literary by any stretch of the
imagination, he was a businessman—would read to me. He had
Darío's complete works and he'd read the poems out loud. I
was fascinated listening to him, without understanding a word.

• *How old were you then?*

Ernesto: Six or seven. I was six. Later I remember telling people
I'd invented two poems of my own. I didn't write them down; I
knew them by heart. And my aunts, the older people in the
household, would get me to recite them. One was about Darío's
grave, in León. Probably fairly incoherent—those poems you
hope no one will ever dig up! I also remember that I used to go
out into the courtyard of that childhood home of mine and
string words together, words that rhymed: *rosa, mariposa,
hermosa, fosa* [rose, butterfly, beautiful, ditch]. Just rhyming.
Probably influenced by Darío who had so much rhyme in his
poetry, the poetry I heard from my father.

Later, when I learned to read, I remember lying on the porch
of the same house, reading Darío from that complete works my
father had—there were something like twenty volumes; it was
the Spanish edition, the first complete Darío published—and I
was fascinated once more, though I didn't understand most of
the words. A great aunt of mine used to tell me she'd known

Darío, there in León, but she never understood his poetry. She liked Spanish poetry, she said, and Darío had come along with a "modern" verse she never did get.

• *And I was going to ask you, at some point soon, how you moved from the influence of someone like Darío into your own voice: much more modern, open, conversational,* exteriorista *as you later termed it.*

Ernesto: The thing is, I was never really influenced by Darío. I simply discovered, in Darío, the magic of words. And I began making meaningless verse. Later, at school, when I studied with the Jesuits, I began writing poetry. I was about nine then. And that poetry was clearly influenced by the terrible things they gave us to read, or they gave *me* to read, at least, at schools like those: the romantic Spanish poets, Zorría, and so forth.

When we talked once before you asked me about Carlos Martínez Rivas and Pablo Antonio Cuadra.[2] Pablo Antonio is my cousin, ten years older than I am. They had his first book, *Poemas nicaragüenses* [*Nicaraguan Poems*], at home, and when I learned to read, that was another book I liked going through. It was *vanguardista* [from the vanguard literary movement], but it used a very real language, words from the Nicaraguan countryside, the language of Chontales, "the dead cow," all those poems . . . I didn't understand it all, some of the *vanguardista* images were lost on me, but I liked a lot of what I found there. I remember Pablo Antonio came to stay at our house once, and I had tremendous respect for him because I knew he was a poet. And I knew Carlos Martínez Rivas from the time we were nine or ten, at the Central American School where we both studied. We've been friends ever since.

Carlos and I started out writing together, but we were both writing very awkward verse, the kind of thing young kids wrote at that time. The real poet at our school was Pedro Joaquín

2. Carlos Martínez Riva and Pablo Antonio Cuadra are two of the great Nicaraguan poets living today. Martínez, in spite of his great talent, has begun to publish in Nicaragua in book form only since the advent of the revolution. Cuadra is perhaps the only important Nicaraguan poet who does not support the revolution. He is one of the editors of *La Prensa.*

Chamorro.[3] He was a year ahead of us, he knew a lot more
grammar, he was writing poetry with meter and all, and for us
he was a master. Carlos Martínez and I really looked up to him.
But later Pedro Joaquín stopped writing poetry; it was just
those first years, when he was very young. Carlos Martínez
made his big leap when he was around fourteen. At the age of
fourteen, Carlos was already writing very original poetry, something very different from what the rest of us were able to produce. He was influenced by Neruda, but by the early Neruda,
Crepusculario and so forth. He'd been to Costa Rica and had
access to literature we didn't have.

- *At that point you didn't yet know Coronel,[4] did you?*

Ernesto: No. I met Coronel when I was sixteen. He was an
uncle of mine. And my grandmother, who was his aunt (his
mother's sister), admired him a lot. Because my grandmother
was something of an intellectual. Of the Urtecho family, she
was the one who most admired Coronel. Listening to her talk
was how I first heard about him, and one day I went and
showed him some poems I'd written. As a matter of fact,
Coronel didn't believe I'd written them; he thought they were
by Father Angel Martínez, who was a Jesuit teacher of Carlos
Martínez's and mine at school. Coronel said the Jesuits liked to
write poems and pretend they'd been written by their students.
Angel Martínez actually was an influence on me at that time.
And the poems weren't bad, for a sixteen year old. Later Coronel
began coming by the school, to talk to Carlos Martínez and to
me. And we began writing seriously. Our major influences then
were Alberti, Lorca and Neruda.

- *Not Vallejo?*

---

3. Pedro Joaquín Chamorro, important among the bourgeois opposition to
all the Somozas, edited *La Prensa*. He was murdered by Tacho Somoza on
January 10, 1978.

4. José Coronel Urtecho, one of Nicaragua's most important poets, some
twenty years older than Cardenal and a lifelong mentor, lives in the Río San
Juan area.

Ernesto: We didn't read Vallejo till a year or so later. Vallejo hadn't been published yet. Vallejo died unknown, really, except for his close circle of friends. We were reading what was available to us at the time: Alberti's *Marinero en tierra [Landed Sailor]*, Neruda's *Veinte poemas de amor y una canción desesperada [Twenty Love Poems and a Song of Desperation]*; the early works by those great poets. Later it was Coronel who introduced us to Vallejo, who had just been published in Mexico. His *España, aparta de mí esta cáliz [Spain, Take this Cup from Me]* was another great treasure for us.

Later there were influences from other languages; we began reading Rilke, Proust, Gide, the French poets, and poetry from the United States that Coronel gave us. He'd read us American and English poetry, translating as he went along. Afterward, he began doing serious translations, and each time he finished one he'd bring it around for us to see. And I began to feel a certain influence from that poetry of the United States.

When I finished high school I talked to my parents into letting me go to Mexico to study literature. I wanted to study North American literature. Ernesto Mejía Sánchez had joined our group by that time, and our mentors were Coronel, Pablo Antonio, and Joaquín Pasos (though we saw much less of Joaquín; he was already quite ill by then). So Mejía Sánchez and I went to Mexico and we began to study English-language literature there. But we quickly saw we couldn't really understand it, with the level of English they taught, so we switched over to the department of Spanish literature. But when I finished my studies in Mexico I convinced my parents to send me to the United States, to study American literature. I went with that in mind.

• *Those were your Columbia University years?*

Ernesto: Yes, 1947 through '49. I was at Columbia, in New York City. The first year was mainly just learning English, and beginning to read the poetry as well. And the poet who most influenced me, in whom I discovered the most, was Ezra Pound. His *Cantos*. I remember that the first large edition of *Cantos* came out around then. And my great discovery there was that poetry could be made from anything: anecdotes, texts by other writers, letters, news items, historical chronicles. You could put anything and everything into a poem just like you could in prose. Poetry didn't have to limit itself to a certain kind of vocabulary or a certain theme. You could write poetry about agriculture, politics, history, things you remembered . . .

• *Ernesto, what was your first published book? Not the first book you wrote, necessarily, but the first you published?*

Ernesto: I published quite late. Because when I went with the Trappists, I still hadn't published a book of poems. When I returned to Nicaragua after studying in the United States, and after a trip to Europe I made when I'd finished at Columbia, I began to write *Epigramas [Epigrams]* and some long historical poems. One was about [William] Walker's war on Nicaragua; another was called "Squire in Nicaragua" and uses things Squire told of his experiences in the country as well as a lot that Squire didn't say but I took from other authors or invented myself (Squire wrote that famous book of chronicles about Nicaragua in the nineteenth century). Then I began writing political poetry. And *La hora cero [Zero Hour]*. That was the last poem I wrote before going to Gethsemani, or the last poem I finished, because I wrote it over a period of time.

• Epigramas, *the long historical poems, and then* Gethsemani, Kentucky, *are all from that period then?*

Ernesto: There's a time span. I returned to Nicaragua at the age of twenty-five, and went with the Trappists when I was thirty-one. So there were those six years at home, when I wrote historical and political poems, and epigrams of a political nature and also about love.

• *The famous poems for Claudia . . .*

Ernesto: Yes. When I left the Trappists, my first two books were published in Mexico: *Epigramas* and *La hora cero.* But the manuscripts were already several years old. I'd been publishing in magazines, but I couldn't publish the political epigrams, for example, even outside Nicaragua under my own name. Because under Somoza García's dictatorship, press censorship was much worse than under the other Somozas. The other Somozas were forced to let up to some extent. They allowed at least veiled attacks in *La Prensa.* But Somoza García wouldn't even tolerate a joke. During his first years in power he even forced the opposition papers to publish articles in his favor. A paper could be closed down indefinitely for the slightest uncomplimentary allusion to his person. *La Prensa* was closed down, I remember, because it published a tiny note in which they said the First Lady hadn't been able to attend a Catholic Action meeting because she was at the beach. They saw that as an attack. And that was enough to close the paper! So I had to publish my political poetry under a pseudonym, and I sent them to a number of countries . . .

• *What was your pseudonym?*

Ernesto: "Anonymous Nicaragua." When someone came through—I remember Manuel Scorza came, the Peruvian writer who was just killed in that plane crash in Madrid; he liked some of my poems and he took them with him. Neruda published them in Chile, in a magazine he was putting out, but he never knew who had written them.

• *Ernesto, we've talked about some of your literary influences, or the writers who awakened in you certain levels of consciousness about the poem. What about the revolution? What effect has the struggle of the Nicaraguan people, the whole revolutionary process, had on your work?*

Ernesto: I was always obsessed by my hatred of Somoza. From the first Somoza. And I always wanted to write political poetry, attacking Somoza; it was something I felt so deeply I had to express it. But I couldn't figure out how to do that. There didn't seem to be any models for writing political poetry. I didn't want to write propaganda, tracts . . . I wanted it to be poetry. I wanted it to be poetic and political at the same time. The first poem I

wrote that satisfied me poetically *and* politically is one of the
epigrams: "En la tumba del guerillero" [At the Guerrilla's Tomb].
Years later, Carlos Mejía Godoy[5] put it to music.

That's an important poem for me, not just because it's my first
successful political poem, but because I wrote it when taking
part in a conspiracy—a great deal has been said about this event—
the April Conspiracy. It was a plan we had to take the presidential palace, capture Somoza, and take power.

• *That was 1954 . . .*

Ernesto: Nineteen fifty-four. I was very close to one of the
leaders of the plan, one of its martyrs: Adolfo Báez Bone. I'd
written that poem of mine for Sandino, and the idea was that no
one knew where the guerrilla was buried but the whole country
was his tomb. And I was thinking of showing it to Báez Bone; I
thought he'd like it. Báez Bone was an officer in the army, a
tremendously charismatic figure, much loved by the people.
And Somoza was afraid of him. He was a born leader. In our
political group he was the contact inside the army.

This group was made up of Pedro Joaquín Chamorro, Rafael
Córdoba Rivas, Reinaldo Teffel, and Arturo Cruz, among
others.[6] When he got out of prison—for he'd served a prison
term—Báez Bone became our leader. I was thinking of showing
him my poem at our next meeting, but our next meeting turned
out to be the one at which they told us we were going to attack
the presidential palace!

That action failed. The principal leaders were captured and
assassinated. They cut Pablo de Leal's tongue out. They say they
castrated Báez Bone. And one of the two is supposed to have

5. Carlos Mejía Godoy is a Nicaraguan composer and singer whose music—
traditional, folk, and protest—has accompanied his people's struggle over the
past decade. "The Peasant Mass" as well as the FSLN anthem are his.
    6. Pedro Joaquín Chamorro has already been mentioned. Rafael Córdoba
Rivas, a member of the Conservative Party, is today a member of Nicaragua's
governing Junta. Reinaldo Teffel, a prominent member of the Christian movement, is president of the Nicaraguan Institute of Welfare and Social Security.
    Arturo Cruz, ex-member of the Junta, now works with the counter-revolu-
tionary movement against Nicaragua.

stained Tacho Somoza's shirt with his blood. That's the old Somoza's son. He was the main torturer. In any case, they were tortured to death. Others of the group were taken prisoner; others took asylum in different embassies; others went into hiding. I went into hiding.

Later mutual friends of Báez Bone's and mine said why didn't I dedicate that poem about the guerrilla's tomb to him instead of to Sandino. Sandino was a well-known figure, they said, while Báez Bone was relatively unknown. And no one knew where he had died, either, nor where he was buried. He was an unknown hero and martyr; no one knew where his body was. I gave the poem a new name, "Epitaph for Adolfo Báez Bone's Tomb." And I began to feel I had found a way of writing political poetry. So I kept on writing political epigrams, along with the epigrams that were love poems.

One of the cantos in *Zero Hour* is about that April conspiracy. Another is about Sandino. And *Zero Hour* was going to be a much longer poem; I was going to write a lot more about Sandino, for example, when it was cut short by my religious conversion. I was going to write about all the struggles in Nicaraguan history, about the struggle against *yanqui* imperialism, against the succession of Somozas; it was almost endless what I had in mind.

• *Ernesto, I want to ask you to talk about your religious conversion. You were born and raised a Catholic, and yet you speak of your decision as a conversion. I know it's one of the really important moments in your experience, and as I've come to understand the religiosity of the Nicaraguan people as a whole, and the importance of faith in their lives, I've come to realize that your decision might be called prophetic. You knew from an early age that you were a poet, and you might have gone on to exercise one of the various professions common to poets: university professor, editor, something like that. But you decided to commit yourself to a religious life. How did that happen?*

Ernesto: It's something I felt from the time I was a child. I used to play at saying Mass. In the same way as I was affected from an early age by poetry, I also had a great religious inclination. When I was a child I used to say I was going to be a priest when

I grew up. But when I began to write, seriously write, I didn't want to give that up. That was when I began to feel a certain conflict, what to do with my life. I always felt like I was doing something I shouldn't be, or that I wasn't doing exactly what I should.

• *Did the poetry seem incompatible with a religious life?*

Ernesto: It wasn't just the poetry; I had to reject marriage, freedom . . . maybe not poetry as such, but poetry meant women to me, my great desire to love a woman, and that seemed to be my greatest obstacle to choosing a religious life. I had several relationships with women, but I always felt that if I married I'd have to give up that which seemed to me to be my true calling. God kept on searching me out, tracking me down.

Finally I decided to give in to that call. I'd read San Juan de la Cruz, where he speaks of the total rejection, giving up everything until you come to a total nothingness. And that nothingness is the encounter with God. And I got to the point where I decided to give it a try. It was a kind of suicide: emptying myself of everything, until I felt that God was filling me. Nothing else mattered then; nothing attracted me except that of which I had become enamored: God.

Rigoberto López Pérez shot Somoza García in September of 1956.[7] A few months earlier, I experienced my conversion. And I wanted to enter a Trappist monastery. I'd read Thomas Merton from the time I was at Colombia—when his first books came out—and I'd kept on reading him. I'd even translated some of his poetry. And the only Trappist monastery I knew about was Gethsemani, Kentucky, where Merton was. So I wrote, asking for information about the possibility of entering a Trappist monastery somewhere. I never thought it would be in the

---

7. Rigoberto López Pérez was a young patriot (and poet) who coordinated and executed a successful plot against the dictator's life. On September 21, 1956, Rigoberto arrived at a party at the "Workers' House," in León, and shot Somoza García at close range. He was immediately murdered by the bodyguards, and a terrible repression—claiming dozens of lives—descended on the country.

United States. In fact, I explained in my first letter that I was from a tropical climate, and I asked about a monastery where I might be accepted. And they responded by simply sending the application forms.

So I felt God wanted me to go to Gethsemani. And I filled out the forms. I later found out that they rejected almost all of their applicants. Because of Merton, the place received a lot of publicity, and they were very strict about whom they accepted. Most of the novices stayed a few days at most, and then they left. The Trappist life-style was a very hard one. Men came there out of romanticism, out of depression, or neurosis. One of the requirements was that you had to see a psychiatrist.

I filled out the forms, and I later found out that the abbot, when he received my first letter, had told Merton: "Write that man from Nicaragua and tell him not to come." Since they rejected almost everyone, he said, "That one from South America, he's from another culture, another climate; he'll never make it here." And then Merton told me that he heard a voice, absolutely clear, telling him I should be admitted. So he ignored what the abbot had told him, and he sent me the papers. Merton told me that much later, after I'd left the Trappists, when I went back once to visit him, after my ordination as a priest.

I entered the Trappist monastery without having published a book. I knew it was an antiliterary order, that Merton was an exception among the Trappists. Since the twelfth century, when the Trappists had a great mystic writer, Saint Bernard, I knew they hadn't had another. The order believed that to be a monk in their community one shouldn't write or in any other way bring attention to oneself. The idea was to bury yourself for life.

The Trappist life was the life of a peasant. You worked in the fields. So I entered the monastery aware of the fact that I wouldn't be able to write, and one of the first things Merton told me when I arrived was that the abbot had said I must renounce my vocation as a poet. I told Merton I knew I'd have to renounce everything, and I was willing to do so. He told me he thought they were soon going to prohibit his writing, as well. "It's good to be able to accept that," he said. He also told me it was possible that at some future date I would be allowed to write again. "For now, it's not possible. You can take notes, but you cannot write professionally. Nor think of publishing."

I took many notes the two years I was there, and later, after I'd left, those notes became the basis for my Trappist poems. They were the record of simple experiences: what happened in a day, things that occurred to me, landscapes. So they're very simple poems, simple and objective. When I left Gethsemani my first books came out: *Los epigramas, La hora cero,* and a bit later, *Gethsemani, Kentucky.*

At Gethsemani I suffered from headaches that became worse as the time passed. They've never really left me; I've had them for thirty years now. The Trappist life is hard, as I said; it's like army life. Everything is regulated, down to the minute. You get up at 2:00 in the morning, and at 2:05 you have to be on your way to the choir. They give you five minutes to wash your face, brush your teeth. The first chants begin at 2:10, and there's severe punishment for those who are half a minute late.

That's the way it was, all day long, till you went to bed at seven. My headaches made it more and more difficult for me to participate fully. One day it was the choir I couldn't attend; the next day I couldn't work in the fields. Until another monk, who had been a doctor, said I couldn't continue there. I resisted that decision, even though I was sick, but Merton said I'd probably have to resign myself to spending my life in an infirmary. It was ridiculous, he said, because it seemed it had to do with nervous tension. And that perhaps another kind of life would enable me to get rid of those headaches. (Though I've never gotten rid of them, with any of the various life-styles I've had.)

Merton told me to try the Benedictines. And that's why I went to Cuernavaca. But at the same time, Merton was planning on leaving the Trappists. He wanted to found a different order, a different kind of community, and we planned on doing that together. He'd thought, at first, of the Virgin Islands. He'd seen a book with pictures of the Virgin Islands and was taken with them. It's a good thing he never went there; he would have been disappointed. There's not much virgin about those islands.

Later Merton began to think of Latin America, and particularly Nicaragua: the Río San Juan area, or the lake. The island of Ometepe perhaps. He also thought of the Andes, but he was pretty much decided on Nicaragua. And when I had to leave he said it was providential—that's the language we used—that it was the will of God that I leave, because it would be easier for me to found the community that way. If I'd waited to take my final vows, it would have been much more difficult.

Merton felt it was important that I become a priest. That way, if it were impossible for him to leave the Trappists, I could found the community without him. And as it turned out, he wasn't able to leave. After my ordination, I went back to visit him at Gethsemani, and that's when he told me about the inspiration he'd had years before, the clear voice telling him it was important they receive me there. And he felt, as I did, that my two years at the monastery were important. Important in terms of my formation.

• *You'd never worked the land until you went to Kentucky?*

Ernesto: No. That's where I learned to work the land with my hands, drenched with sweat in those hot Kentucky Augusts, or in the rain, or the snow of winter. That kind of experience was to do me in good stead for Solentiname, later on. Well, the rest of the story you know: I always thought my life had been a coherent line, set forth by God, a series of experiences that may seem crazy and disconnected to many: burying myself alive in a Trappist monastery, then twelve years on an island at Solentiname (where many also thought it was a waste of time, a place unknown even *inside* Nicaragua), and then the revolution, my exile which meant traveling around the world doing solidarity work for my country, and finally this very bureaucratic job as Minister of Culture, with its own round of voyages since the victory.

About the time I went to Solentiname, there was a contest on the radio here, and one of the questions was "Where is Solentiname?" There was a prize for the person who phoned in with the right answer. That'll give you an idea of what an isolated place it is!

As Minister of Culture, for the most part I've had to renounce my vocation as a poet. Yet it all seems like a single mission to me: the total silence of the Trappist novitiate, where you communicate only through sign language; the isolation of Solentiname, and the agitated activity of these trips, before and after the revolution. Everything up to now has been a preparation, helping me give myself to this cause.

• *Ernesto, during the time you were at Solentiname, it seems to me that your poetry reached the level of your major work:* "Oración por Marilyn Monroe" [Prayer for Marilyn Monroe], "Oráculo sobre Managua" [Oracle over Managua], "El canto nacional" [The National Song] . . . *Those are all poems from that period, aren't they?*

Ernesto: There was an evolution. I kept on writing different kinds of poetry, narrative poems, historical and political poems, and instead of love poems to women I wrote a poetry of mystic love. And I continued to write about the [American] Indians. I first became interested in the Indians through Merton, who greatly admired those cultures. Merton used to say that the Indians were more truly religious than the young American novices at the monastery . . . he said the novices didn't even have any passion. And how could you be religious without passion?

Merton was very anti-American. He was born in France, and his first language was French. But then he came to the United States, and of course he was an American. But he always hated the American way of life. And it colored everything he thought and did. He thought Latin American poetry was better than U.S. poetry, while I believed the opposite, that U.S. poetry was better than our own. He used to say his own poetry was more French than American, but I don't think that was true. Everything about the United States was bad, according to Merton; perhaps that's why he wanted to found a community in Latin America. He was obsessed by Latin America, although toward the end of his life he began to change that obsession for one with the Orient, Zen Buddhism, and so forth.

Merton used to say that real mysticism, real wisdom, could be found in the forgotten cultures. So when I left the Trappists I began to do a lot of reading about the Indians, both of North and South America. And I wrote quite a few poems about the Indians. But I was talking about the evolution in my own poetry: it began, basically, as a poetry of protest against Somoza and against *yanqui* imperialism. Then perhaps it was more directly against the whole capitalist system. And after my experience in Cuba, my poetry became more Marxist-oriented. And I began to study Marxism.

• *I remember that first trip to Cuba, and the second. How impressed you were with the struggles and achievements of the Cuban people, and the shock it caused in Managua; when you came back and said you were a socialist, let alone a Marxist! Yet your experience fit right in with similar experiences other committed religious people were having throughout Latin America. And how that was reflected at the meetings in Medellín and Puebla, following the Second Vatican Council.* [8] *But there was also a great influence of pacifism in your work in those years, Ernesto. I remember, during the Mexican years, how much Gandhi meant to you.*

Ernesto: That was Merton's influence, too. Because Merton was very Gandhian, he'd read a lot of Gandhi and he eventually became involved in the great pacifist movement that took hold in the United States, against atomic war. He wrote a good many articles; he became something of a leader in that movement against the arms race, against nuclear war. The abbot even went so far as to prohibit him writing against war! For a time he mimeographed what he was writing, and sent it out to close friends.

8. Pope John XXIII's Second Vatican Council—initiated, interestingly enough, in the same year (1961) that the FSLN was being founded in Nicaragua—gave rise to important meetings of Latin American bishops (Medellín, Colombia, in 1968, and Puebla, Mexico, in 1979). The two major breakthroughs for the Catholic Church, to come out of these events, were the acceptance of the Church as something inside history, and the assumption, as Christians, of a "preferential option for the poor." Both brought Christians and revolutionaries closer together than they had ever been.

• *Ernesto, do you think your transit from a pacifist position to an acceptance of the need for armed struggle comes out of your experience in Cuba—which clearly was tremendously important to you—or simply from being a Nicaraguan and seeing the way the struggle developed in your country?*

Ernesto: No, it was the Nicaraguan experience. What happened to everyone here. Around 1968 I had my first meeting with Tomás Borge. Later I met with Carlos Fonseca, and again with Tomás and Carlos together. Those meetings were naturally underground; and we had long, long discussions, in which violence was always an issue. From the beginning I agreed with everything they said, with the program they outlined—the way they wanted to change society, everything. But I thought the method should be the one Gandhi used: nonviolence.

In any case, I told them, as a priest I cannot take part in armed struggle. That was our discussion, from the beginning. I was totally frank and open with them, and they were extremely tolerant with me. Very patient, I'd say. Because they knew I was wrong, but never tried to force me. We just kept on talking, and gaining each other's confidence. I even lent Carlos a biography of Gandhi, a book I read a great deal at Solentiname: the Louis

Fischer biography. And when he returned it, he told me had learned to admire Gandhi greatly. But that he was more than ever convinced that armed struggle was the only way. Because in India, even after Gandhi's struggle, the people were still miserable. Whereas in China a different kind of struggle had brought freedom for the people.

I considered myself a member of the FSLN from the time I accepted my first mission: going to the Russell Tribunal, in Rome, in 1976. The organization sent me to denounce the beastly crimes being committed against the peasantry here. When the war ended, I thought I would be able to go back to live on the island. After all those years of struggle, so much traveling and exile, underground and agitation, I dreamed of returning to Solentiname, rebuilding the community and writing the chronicle of this revolution. But the revolution had other plans for me.

It was Father D'Escoto who called me in Costa Rica to ask if I'd accept a cabinet post as Minister of Culture. I said I didn't much like the idea, but that if it was an order, I'd accept. He asked me again, "Do you accept?" and again I said if it was an order I'd have to. "But do you accept?" he insisted. And I finally said, "Yes."

• *Some of the seeds planted at Solentiname have been the basis for much of the work the Ministry of Culture has promoted: the poetry workshops, primitive painting, crafts. Back in the sixties and seventies, when you were in the community, did you ever think you'd be able to extend those experiences throughout the country?*

Ernesto: I didn't even imagine the poetry workshops would work at Solentiname. I didn't think that peasants, with such a low cultural level, could really understand anything but the simplest verse. It was Mayra Jiménez, a poet from Costa Rica, who came to the community at one point, who initiated the workshop experience. She had done something like that with children in her own country. I didn't even come to the workshop she started at Solentiname until it had been going for a while. And she invited me to read some of my poems. I saw that many of the peasants were writing really fine verse, as well as learning how to understand and criticize that of others.

As the community evolved, we started with the painting and the crafts. The experience through the Ministry of Culture has been extraordinary. In so many areas. Right now, for instance, the *Piñata*, or fair of Nicaraguan handicrafts and goods. Or the Corn Fair in the spring. So many activities born of the people's traditions and creativity! You ask me to sum up what I feel the influence of our revolution has been on Nicaraguan culture: it's released that culture, given it its freedom! And this is something that just keeps on growing; it's infinite!

During our conversation, Ernesto attended to two telephone calls his secretary deemed important enough to justify interruption. One call clearly required his presence at a meeting later that day. The other brought him the voice of his old friend Bosco Centeno, one of the young peasants at Solentiname, now a captain with the Sandinista People's Army, with responsibility in the defense of the Río San Juan area. "How are things in the south?" the poet-priest asked the poet-soldier.[9] And then Bosco's answer broke into a smile across Ernesto's face: "When are we going to find time for that fish you were telling me about?"

The year 1983 is coming to a close. One of the recent and enormously complex tasks undertaken by the Ministry of Culture was that of storing underground the nation's entire cultural patrimony: works of art, archives, historic documents—important elements in a people's identity. The invasion, which seemed imminent, would not catch Nicaraguans with its people's treasures exposed and vulnerable. At the same time, living cultural events—theater, exhibitions, readings, music, the National Circus season—continue and multiply.

The Minister of Culture will retire for a few days, over Christmas and New Year's, to his beloved island. The year 1984 promises more challenges . . . and work. As Ernesto says, "This is something that just keeps on growing; it's infinite!"

---

9. Bosco Centeno won a national poetry prize last year for his first book of verse.

Michele Najlis

Risking a somersault in the air

"I remember writing my first poem when I was about fifteen. We were a pretty tight little group; Fernando Gordillo and Sergio Ramirez—although they're both a bit older than I am —and Luis Rocha. I think it was Luis who gave me my first books of poetry, got me reading poetry for the first time. It was through him that I got to know Ernesto Cardenal. I read his *Epigrams.*"

I am at Michele Najlis's house. She's a poet, critic, woman, mother—a surprising being whose presence evokes both the legendary and the everyday. I remember an image of Michele from the sixties, when I received—in Mexico—a photograph of a slim young woman with penetrating eyes. And I have another image of Michele, in the days just after the victory of the revolution in Nicaragua: serious, heavier, dressed in olive green, and in charge of immigration. Now I contemplate Michele today: reflective, sipping coffee from a simple metal cup, a little pensive perhaps in the presence of the tape recorder and this inquisitive interviewer. But she begins to speak, slowly at first and then with growing animation.

"I was fourteen or fifteen then; now I'm thirty-six. So I'm talking about twenty years ago. I was a great admirer of Ernesto's poetry. In fact, he was the first poet to whom I showed my own verse. I remember arriving with my notebook under

my arm. He'd given me an appointment for 10 A.M., and at 9:30
I was pacing back and forth in front of his house, scared to go up
to the door. My first readings? Cardenal, Vallejo—and Vallejo
still has an important literary influence on me today. Later, at
the university, Neruda appeared. And Darío, who was presented to us by the dictatorship in a very distorted way."

We were already talking about Vallejo, Neruda, Darío . . . but
I wanted to hear about Michele's relationship with Fernando
Gordillo, someone who is highly esteemed and at the same time
so relatively little known. So I urged her to go back in time, to
share some memories with me.

Michele: I met Fernando when he was already quite ill with
the disease that was to cause his death. If there was one thing I
admired about him, it was the way in which he consistently
kept up a permanent and dynamic interest in culture. He and
Sergio Ramírez. But Fernando wasn't just an erudite person, he
was up to date on everything being written, and he knew about
other areas of cultural expression as well. At that, we didn't

even think we had a culture of our own, we Nicaraguans. Or if we had one, we weren't aware of it.

The *Ventana* group marked the beginning of our search for our own cultural identity: looking at Darío (in a different way), at Salomón de la Selva . . . In spite of his illness, Fernando kept on going to the university; he even taught classes in a wheel-chair. He was someone who always found a meaning to his life. He gave all he had as a member of the FSLN. And if clandestine political activities were difficult for normal people, you can imagine they meant a double effort and a double risk for him.

Fernando was a very disciplined person. When you went to see him at home you'd find him reading, studying, looking for someone to help him write his stories down, his essays. We all leapt at the chance to help him write, and we'd take turns copying what he dictated, correcting it."

• *Michele, did you yourself participate in* Ventana?

Michele: I was a kind of little sister to *Ventana.* Because when I began to write, comrades like Sergio and Fernando were seven or eight years older than I was. And at that age that was the difference between adolescence and young adulthood. I was the little sister, but greatly indulged and encouraged. I think Sergio is responsible for having published the worst poems I've ever written. He was always so encouraging. Today I read that first issue of *Ventana,* and my poems seem terrible. But who knows if I would have kept on writing if I hadn't had that kind of support. I think young people need a magazine like that, one in which they can experiment and develop their writing skills, without it being something as serious as *Nicarauac* [the official literary magazine of Nicaragua's Ministry of Culture], for example, or as incipient as *Chacalaca* [the magazine published for the People's Culture Houses]. Most of us who are more or less writers today came out of *Ventana.*

• *Michele, tell me a bit about your books. When did* El viento armado [The Wind in Arms] *come out?*

Michele: It came out in 1979, in Guatemala. I always joke about publishing a book of verse every ten years. I don't know if that will be true of a third book, or if I'll write a third book, but it was true with the first two. *El viento armado* is a collection of my poetry from 1958 to 1968, more or less. Sergio was responsible for the edition and did a very nice design for the cover. But the distribution was awful. I think the mice at San Carlos University [in Guatemala] ate about 80 percent of the press run. It was poorly distributed, but was well received by those who saw copies. At least that's what I was told. And there were no reviews, neither good nor bad.

That's one of the saddest things that can happen to a writer. A writer's work is pretty solitary. You shut yourself up behind four walls with paper and a pen, or a typewriter. You don't have the same kind of communication with the public that an actor has, for instance, or a musician. It's not a direct communication. The actor and the musician know if they're reaching people or not. The writer may suppose or intuit that he's communicating, but he needs that response.

Now there's a new edition of that first book published by New Nicaragua, our publishing company. It's been enriched with some very nice drawings by Raquel Villareal, who I think interprets my women's feelings very well. Real women's feelings, not those of "the fragile little woman" they're always associating with women's consciousness. But more our sense of well-being, of flowering.

• *Michele, you're speaking of your feelings as a poet and your feelings as a woman; since the revolution you've held some posts which might not seem to have much to do with being a poet—although in a revolution everything has to do with poetry—you've taken on tasks like being in charge of the first immigration office in the new government. Later, you held other important posts in the Ministry of the Interior. How did those jobs affect you as a poet and as a woman? And what made you decide later on to go back to a field more akin to the world of literature, as a journalist with* El Nuevo Diario?

Michele: There were several things that influenced that whole process. In the first place, I wasn't in Nicaragua during the final years of our liberation struggle. There was a gap, then, in my political development. I missed out on a whole part of our history. I would have liked to have had the experience of being inside Nicaragua at that time, but for a whole series of reasons I had to stay in the rearguard. So I came back to the country just after victory, and that had an important impact. I felt the need of a more direct relationship with the revolutionary reality—almost the opposite of what I had had to do in Costa Rica in those final years, which was precisely to attend the university, to relate to intellectuals, and so forth. I needed the other side. That was part of it.

In the second place, in the euphoria of the victory I don't think many of us asked ourselves, "What do I want to do, as an individual? How am I going to find fulfillment?" That wasn't the problem at that point in time. I was envious, for example, of the men who were building highways. It seemed to me to be the most beautiful work you could do, something so specific, a real symbol of our reconstruction.

I came back to Nicaragua with the idea of working at the Ministry of Culture. I even had an agreement to that effect, with Father Cardenal. But I happened to be at Radio Sandino when I was assigned to a task. In those first few days after the victory, many people had no idea where their sons and daughters were, those who had been combatants. Lots of messages were coming to the radio station from mothers and fathers who wanted to know if their kids were still alive, where they were—and someone got the idea of sending us to the barracks and other places where the comrades were sleeping and making lists of those who were there. I was working on that project, when I ran into Comandante Borge, and right out of the blue he told me to report to the Ministry of the Interior at eight the next morning.

The work they offered me in immigration had high priority at that time. I stayed with the Ministry of the Interior, and was in fact surprised to find that I liked the work at immigration tremendously. It was like creating a being, a whole complex organism, out of nothing. Like Comandante Borge said, it's as if we're inventing a country. Later, when I transferred over to the media control office, there were a lot of tensions. That was a job no one would envy. It was really hard. A while ago, I'm not sure where, I read that people in the United States are bombarded with so much information at one time that they automatically reject more than a certain amount. And the nation literally becomes "smaller" because people feel they are becoming less significant in the midst of an overwhelming amount of information that they can't even assimilate. The average person doesn't even begin to process everything he reads or hears. But in my case, in that job, I had to process everything. It was a very traumatic experience.

Later, I went to Zelaya Norte [northern Zelaya]. I went with the "Omar Torrijos" Brigade, and that was a very important experience for me. As it turned out, we were mobilized in December 1981 during the so-called Red Christmas. I met some incredible people on the brigade. I think I'll always remember our military instructor. Every afternoon, after four or five or six hours of the toughest kind of military training, he'd line us up in platoons and relentlessly tells us: "Only the workers and the peasants will make it." He'd make the same speech every day.

After some ten days of sweating, vomiting, falling down and getting up again, one day this guy finally told us: "Only the workers and peasants will make it . . . and a few intellectuals who embrace the cause of the proletariat." I think that phrase was a great source of pride to the thirty-two comrades who had joined the brigade. We felt we had finally gained that comrade's respect, the respect of someone we ourselves respected so much.

After the brigade, I ended up working on the paper. I find the people at *El Nuevo Diario* to be very understanding, very tolerant of my work. No one ever tells me to write this or that; I have complete freedom there. And on the other hand, the job imposes a certain discipline: two-and-a-half pages of copy a day. And I finally have enough time to do my own writing. I'm struggling with a novel right now. But I don't want to talk about it, because the more I talk about it the less I feel the need to write it.

• *Michele, there's been a pretty polemical discussion these days about the role of the writer in the Nicaraguan Revolution. Writers especially are talking about that, their role, the role of the Ministry of Culture, the role of the ASTC [Sandinista Cultural Workers Association]. Do you have something to say about it all?*

Michele: Well, for me the creation of the Ministry of Culture on July 19, 1979, shows the revolution's political decision from the very beginning, its will to place that kind of importance on culture. And important things have been achieved—above all, with the People's Culture Houses; in the amateur theater movement; with folk dance; ENIGRAC [the recording company], with musicians. The creation and consolidation of INCINE [the film industry] is also far beyond what many of us hoped for.

Where I feel the Ministry of Culture hasn't achieved so much is with our professional artists. Perhaps "professional" isn't the best word. Let's say, those of us who are over thirty. And that's what the ASTC has been called to deal with, and they've made some inroads on the problem. The existence of the ASTC is, again, a sign that the revolution takes its artists seriously. I think the ASTC has made some important gains in the areas of painting, the circus arts, theater, photography, dance. Perhaps we, the writers, are those who have least been able to move in this respect.

But I think writers have a pretty specific problem. In part, it's our class origin. Most of us are from the middle classes, and I think that creates problems for us, even in terms of our identity as artists. It's been harder for us to find our place within the revolution than it has been for other creative people.

It's easy to say the ASTC's to blame, blah blah blah, but the truth is the ASTC calls us together—what are we going to do? what do we writers want?—and we always find ourselves up in the air, so to speak. As if we can figure out what our place in the revolution really is. And of course it's not easy. I find myself thinking at times: Well, what should I do? Sit down and write a novel, or go off with a reserve battalion? Or even concerning more mundane decisions: Should I stay up all night doing guard duty or writing that chapter of the novel that has me so excited?

These are the choices we're forced to make on a daily basis. But aside from this, I think we have to do some convincing of ourselves that writers really are important to the revolution. I don't mean we should consider ourselves more important than anyone else, but it's like that comrade who was building highways at the beginning of the revolution. I think that if we writers could be sure that publishing a book is as important as paving roads, we'd have more confidence in ourselves and then maybe we'd be able to see more clearly how to define ourselves within our union.

On the other hand, it *is* true that we've felt a change, despite our lack of organization or our faulty organization—our lack of collective consciousness, if you will—as a union. Before the revolution in Nicaragua I would never have dared put "writer" on an application form for anything; I'd have put "teacher," "journalist," anything. It would have seemed ridiculous to me to put "writer." But I do it now, and so do many other comrades. The revolution has given us a certain status; maybe we earned it, maybe not. But we feel a greater responsibility.

It's hard to try to find your place as a person who comes from the middle classes within a revolutionary process that you love but which somehow disorients you every day. You remember the bit about only the workers and peasants making it to the end, and we intellectuals running along behind, trying to catch up. And for women from the middle classes, women who in many ways might have had objective reasons for wanting to identify with the bourgeoisie—in spite of which we do the impossible in order to identify with the proletariat—our problems are even worse.

In our case it's not only the matter of finding our identity as writers and as revolutionaries, but as women too, of breaking out from a series of snares inherited by generation after generation of the women, up to the present, and of trying to break that chain, not only in order to be happy ourselves but in order to create the possibility of happiness for our daughters. It's all very interesting, and very difficult. I think it's a challenge for us, as women, and it helps us to understand the thing about proletarian revolution not only meaning the liberation of the workers but of all humanity, and that implies women as women.

The day is growing dark. Michele's coffee cup is empty. Her oldest daughter, still quite small, has come and gone several times; and her mother has explained, gently, "I'm working." I ask the poet if there's anything she'd like to add, and she replies:

Michele: Only to say that my novel is about women in the revolution. I don't know how I'll do it, or even if I'll be able to do it, but it would certainly be a trauma for me if I resigned from the Ministry of the Interior in order to do this novel, and then didn't finish it. I said, Well, I'm going to take the leap and see if I can be a writer or not. It's a bit like risking a somersault in the air, and not knowing if you're going to land on your feet or break your neck. It was a real problem for me, just how confident I was of myself as a writer, and whether or not I was letting the revolution down by resigning from the ministry to try to write.

• *What did the Ministry of the Interior have to say about all that? How did they respond to your request?*

Michele: With a great deal of understanding! My immediate superior was Comandante Omar Cabezas, and he told me, "Go on, get out quick before I get the same idea!"

Omar Cabezas

The thing is, I am the masses

Much has been said about Omar Cabezas (born in León, 1950), about the author of *The Mountain Is Something More than a Great Expanse of Green*, about the Brigade and Guerrilla Commander Omar Cabezas–head of the Nicaraguan Ministry of the Interior's Political Section. His critics and friends talk about him. *Compas*[1] and literary people talk about him. The enemy certainly talks a good deal about him. Omar's people talk about him and listen to him, because, among other things, he's a storyteller, full of life and stories from life.

To listen to him, to talk with him, I arrived at his house outside Managua one morning in July. It was early. He wasn't yet in uniform, and there was no protocol about the way he received me (in fact, Omar is someone who rarely worries about protocol). He was playing with his youngest daughter, and with the rabbits, deer, geese, and other animals inhabiting his garden. He agreed to a "candid" interview. And so we got on with it . . .

Omar: I knew I could write. I always knew that. What I didn't know was if I was going to be "a writer." I always had great confidence in what I was capable of doing, especially when talking with others.

1. *Compas*, comrades.

• *Are you speaking of now, or before?*

Omar: Always. That is, up to the present. I'd say at thirteen I already knew. Even when I was quite young, I remember once when they had me do a composition at school. It must have been fourth grade, something like that. They asked all the kids for a composition, due the following day. It was about "mothers." I went home that day and did my homework, and I wrote the composition. But when I handed it in the next day the teacher gave me a five . . . she said I had copied it.

• *Five was bad?*

Omar: It was bad all right. It was flunking. The worst you could get. In those days grades went from 5 to 10. To pass you had to

have a 7.51 average. I remember the composition didn't take much to do, it wasn't hard for me at all. And it was the first time I had ever sat before a blank piece of paper, to write something personal. I'd never even written a letter to a friend; I was too young to have friends in other cities. So it was the first time I wrote something personal, which wasn't copied or assigned to us in class by the teacher. My composition turned out real well and they gave me a 5 because the teacher said I'd copied. So I told her no, it was mine. That she could ask my papa and mama . . . (*to his mother, who is standing nearby*) Mama, remember that composition the teacher sent back to the house? (*Omar's mother: that was '58, or '60.*) It's something I've never talked about, you see.

• *What authors did you read, as a child?*

Omar: None.

• *You didn't read?*

Omar: No.

• *When did you start reading?*

Omar: When I wanted to change the world. But then I read sociology, Marxism.

• *And when did you decide you wanted to change the world?*

Omar: Well, I knew the world was all wrong since I was just a kid. But I think that all came together for me when my father left my mother.

• *When was that?*

Omar: When I was thirteen. My papa left my mother for another woman. And at that point . . .

• *Did your parents' separation affect you much?*

Omar: Of course. At that point there was a lot of hardship at home. And my mama had to deal with it by herself.

• *How many in your family?*

Omar: Seven.

• *You have six brothers and sisters?*

Omar: I had six brothers. Three of them died in the war. And my papa also died, but that was before. Half my family. My mother and father had seven sons.

• *And all your children are daughters!*

Omar: Yeah, a genetic changeover. Because my brothers all have only daughters too. All my brothers; their children are female. One who was killed in the war left a little girl.

• *So, Omar, when you did begin to read, what were your first books?*

Omar: Well, the first book I read, paradoxically, since we're celebrating the 26th of July this week, was *History Will Absolve Me*.[2] For us Moncada—like Tomás Borge said in his speech—was more than a name. For me, Moncada, when I read the book, wasn't a memorable date. Or, to be more exact, it wasn't *just* a memorable date. Moncada was an old friend. Because the Sandinista National Liberation Front, at that time, wasn't more than forty militants in all of Nicaragua. Can you imagine that? Moncada came to be the justification for our adventure, the argument we needed to prove a revolution was possible. Moncada became an intimate friend, something that gave us our reason for being. When no one believed you were for real, when everyone looked at you as if you were crazy, Moncada was the record of someone who had done it . . . and had triumphed. Moncada was proof it was possible, it was what we needed, a good friend, the person you could share your dreams with. It was our reservoir of hope, our reserve to keep from going under, our point of faith to hang on to.

• *What year are we talking about now?*

Omar: 1968.

---

2.   Fidel Castro's defense after being taken prisoner following the July 26, 1953, attack on Moncada Barracks, in Santiago de Cuba. It contained the Cuban revolutionary movement's entire program for changing society.

• *It's interesting. We're talking about 1968; the Cuban Revolution was nearly ten years old by then. But the important thing for you was Moncada, not the victory, what came later, but the seed, the beginning.*

Omar: Sure. Because they had made their revolution, and we still had ours ahead of us. Moncada came to us here in our period of solitude, like an incredible friend. It made us see that it was possible. For us, Moncada was just what we needed, the glove that fit the hand. This, then, was my first book. The second, strangely enough, was written by a traitor: Carlos Franqui . . .

• *Of course,* The Book of the Twelve. [3]

Omar: *The Book of the Twelve.* That was the other justification. Those books together, were our friendly accomplices.

• *Moncada translated into real people's lives . . . real flesh and blood people.*

Omar: Accomplices. Our friends. And the only people who believed in us. Even though they didn't know us, right? Do you know what I mean?

• *Yes. And literature? Was there any literature that interested you at that time in your life?*

Omar: Well, I read because they assigned us books at the university. That's why I read. My brother read. My oldest brother read the classics. He read *María* by Jorge Isaacs, the *Three Musketeers* by Alexander Dumas. My brother read a lot of literature. And my papa adored literature. But what happened? In my case there was a problem. I read *El Señor Presidente* by Miguel Angel Asturias, and I read *Don Quixote* by Cervantes. But I read them because they were assigned reading, in class. Because I was involved with the FSLN as a youngster, I wasn't even seventeen when I joined, what did I start out reading? Marxism. Because I was sure we were going to change the world. And I'm not saying this out of vanity.

3. *The Book of the Twelve,* by Carlos Franqui. He left Cuba in the sixties and lives in Europe.

- *. . . out of confidence.*

Omar: Exactly. Out of personal confidence. Because I always believed I was capable of moving people, convincing them.

- *Why do you think you believed that; why do you think you had such strong confidence in yourself? A boy coming from a family in which your parents were separated, with severe hardships but not severe poverty, really . . . I mean, what was it that produced that self-confidence in you?*

Omar: Look, there were contradictions in my personality. Because when I was small, I was a runt of a kid, a skinny child, and the ugly duckling of the family. All my brothers were fair, like you, like your kids. My father was fair, too. But my mother wasn't. My mama is Indian, *mestiza*. And my father was white. I came out like my mama. I was small, skinny, physically weak. Physical weakness gives you a certain sense of fragility, on the outside. Especially at school, and in the neighborhood, with the kids in the street.

- *. . . especially being male.*

Omar: Especially being male. So, initially I had a complex about being small, about being weak. Not an inferiority complex, but a sense of my own weakness. At the same time I had the sense that I wasn't dumb. That's why I say there were contradictions. Those things that go on inside kids. I always believed I understood things better than other people, I thought I had more of an ability to learn. And I grew up believing that when I wanted something, by talking to people I could convince them. I always had a certain talent for histrionics. For theater. For acting. People believed I was doing something real. And it was a lie; it was pure imagination. It was clear in my mind, in my head: I knew I was capable of getting what I wanted. And that kind of balanced out my physical weakness. At the university, for instance, I had an imaginary dog. When I was seventeen, eighteen years old. I was always playing around with my imaginary dog. Until one day it was run over by a car.

- *Was the car imaginary, too?*

Omar: I guess so. If the dog was imaginary, the car had to be imaginary too. I remember I used to come home with my dog and my mama thought I was crazy. I'd play around like that, just to bug my mama, to kid her, to make her laugh.

• *I'm still wondering if it's possible for a real car to run over an imaginary dog, or if it has to be an imaginary car that runs over an imaginary dog.*

Omar: I don't know. Maybe a real car could run over an imaginary dog, but in this case I invented the car that killed him. Then again, maybe it was a real car, and I didn't know it. The thing is, I came home with the dog on his leash, right? I'd come with my hand out like this, huh? "This here dog . . ." "What dog?" "This one! You don't have a sense of humor!" I'd say. It was a joke of mine, a goof. So when we were eating, I'd grab a piece of meat and throw it on the floor. "It's for my dog," I'd say. And I loved watching my mama, who didn't really get the joke. Even real serious people like Roberto Huembes, Juan José Quezada, Leonel Rugama[4]—who, in the beginning, resented the whole thing about my dog—afterwards they became real fond of it. And they'd borrow the dog from me and take it to their houses. They'd keep it for a couple of days and then give it back to me. Pure craziness. It was a group craziness, that I invented.

• *You loaned your dog to Leonel?*

Omar: Yeah. I even remember one time I loaned him something of mine, and he never gave it back. I was bugging him to return it to me, a book or something, and he tells me: "That son of a bitch dog destroyed it!" So, what happened? Classes: mathematics, biology, assigned readings, whatnot . . . I read books for all those things. But because I joined up with the FSLN, and since I knew I was going to change the world, I hated all mediocrity. I couldn't go on wanting to change the world and be ignorant or superficial. I hated then, and I still hate,

4. Roberto Huembes, Juan José Quezada and Leonel Rugama were three friends of Omar's, members of the FSLN who became heroes and martyrs of the Nicaraguan Revolution. They were killed at different moments during the insurrectional years.

superficial discourse, and clichés. It just gets to me. So, I started
to read Marxism. I read the first two volumes of Marx's *Capital.*

• *Alone, or with other* compañeros?

Omar: Alone and with others, too. I read the *Anti-Dühring.* I
don't know if you remember, but there were two things that
came out at the same time in Latin America. There was Chile,
the Chilean School of Political Economy; there was that famous
school of sociology in Venezuela—at the Central University, it
was run by someone named Losada Aldama. Then there was
that group of Brazilians doing sociology, with André Gunder
Frank at their head: Teotonio Dos Santos, and those people.
There was the Mexican School of Sociology, too, with Pablo
González Casanova. [Eduardo] Galeano was coming out with
Open Veins of Latin America. So you had that explosion of sociology and political thought in Latin America at that time. The
dependence thesis was part of that. And a whole string of terms
and concepts that exist to this day: the concept of the metropolis
and the periphery.

• *The term "third world" comes from that time.*

Omar: That's right; "third world." So, at least in León,
Nicaragua—which was my universe as well as my Macondo—
there was something else that charged into our world, swept in
like a tornado, through the university, through the literary
circles, and I was at the very center of that tornado, and it was
the Latin American "literary boom." At the same time as we
joined the FSLN, at the same time as we began reading sociology
and Marxism and political thoughts of all kinds, the "boom"
came on the scene with all the force of García Márquez, Vargas
Llosa, *Hopscotch* [by Julio Cortázar], ratata ratata, *A Change of
Skin* by Carlos Fuentes, ta ta ta ta, *The Death of Artemio Cruz,* ta
ta. And so thinking people made a choice. They opted for what
they wanted to read. I mean, I could have chosen literature, I
could have chosen to get into the "boom" world; but I made a
conscious decision that I was going to study Marxism and sociology. I took it upon myself to read every single book of sociology I
could get my hands on. I don't remember a single sociology

book published at that time I didn't read. I even criticized the other comrades. Not Leonel, because Leonel could read all the "boom" writers; he already knew Marxism. But I criticized the others. I told them they shouldn't be reading that "dumb stuff," that they should be reading Marxism and revolutionary writing. So that's why I didn't read. I don't remember having read a book, aside from what they assigned me in class, that wasn't Marxism or sociology.

• *And today?*

Omar: Today . . . well, I read other books, literature . . . and I began when I was in the mountains. But it was forced on me there, too, in a way. Because there weren't any other books, and since I knew how to read and write, I read. It wasn't even like aesthetic recreation. Just general recreation. Because I knew how to read, I could do that. It was a primitive thing. Like simply doing something because there it was, and you knew how to do it. Like a pool player, who suddenly comes across a pool table, so he starts playing pool. That's how I came upon *Unfinished Poems;* and here's something else I've only told one other person, and it's important in terms of the influences I've had: the biggest influence I had was my father. My father was a clever man, an outgoing man, very bold; he got around people, he was very sharp mentally. And he had big dreams. He was in love with development, with progress, and so he was in love with the United States of America. At least back then. Later he changed, and he died a Sandinista. But back then he admired the North Americans' conquest of space. He had a *Readers Digest* culture; he had nearly a thousand *Readers Digests,* he bought them every week. His was a *Life Magazine* culture. He bought *Life* every week. He loved all that. But even so, he was a guy who hated mediocrity. He was one of a kind. So much so, that in León, Nicaragua, in the sixties, he fell in love with a fifteen-year-old girl and moved out of the house to live with her. And they threw him out of the Christian Parents Association, because he was president of that. He was a prestigious man, an opponent of Somoza; and yet he needed to do that, and he went and did it. And that was something in León, a real scandal. My father was a man who was capable of taking a stand.

• *But I don't want you to forget what happened in the mountains . . . that important influence you mentioned.*

Omar: I'm getting to that. The first big influence I had, even as a writer, was my papa. Because my papa wrote books, even though he didn't really write them. He was a charmer. My papa, when he spoke, spoke so richly. He was a storyteller. And when he wrote letters, even business letters, they were wonderful, works of art. But the second influence was when I got to the mountains and began reading Roque Dalton. In *Unfinished Poems.* It was incredible. At first I thought Roque wrote like Leonel. But then I discovered Roque came first, and so I had to admit that Leonel wrote like Roque. I mean, if I was influenced by Leonel, I was really influenced by Roque Dalton as well. Leonel's way of playing around, it was a whole style he had, a way of talking, a way of having fun, a way of being. Each of us, with his particular personality, left his mark on the group, on the collective. Leonel had his way of being, and as far as I knew, he never knew Roque Dalton. I don't think they knew each other. So I discovered that Roque was like Leonel, but then I realized it was the other way around. Leonel was like Roque. Leonel was influenced by Roque. And one of the people who had influenced me most was Leonel Rugama. He left his mark on certain aspects of my conduct. Leonel added certain nuances to my personality. I was influenced by Leonel but not in a literary way . . . in my life. Something more universal than literature. I was influenced by Leonel's personality. It stands to reason that when I wrote I was writing *my* personality, or writing *with my personality,* and so there's something of Leonel there too. I feel that I'm strongly influenced by Leonel Rugama and by my papa, but in neither case in a purely literary way.

• *But for you, Omar, literature isn't simply literature. Your literature is life. So your influences have to be vital influences. I think . . .*

Omar: That's the word I was looking for! Vital, a vitality. That's the word. That's what I wanted to say. It's not a writing style or a narrative style; it's a life-style, a way of thinking, of making things happen, of discovering the *feeling* in things.

• *Omar, at any time before the victory, did you dream of writing the book you later wrote? Or did you simply dream about the victory?*

Omar: I don't know. These are like childhood memories. And this time I'm going to give you an anecdote from my adolescence, because it actually has something to do with what you're asking. Once we climbed a mountain. I think it was San

Cristobal. Night came, and it's a volcano with huge steep rocky passes, gigantic jaws, bigger than this whole house, wider, higher, and with tremendous rocks down below. Night came and we were up there at the top. And how were we supposed to get down? We were Boy Scouts, and a priest had taken us up. We started going down, in single file, one of us leading with a flashlight. There was that light in the dark, the sound of tiny pebbles crunching against the sand; it was like a march of giants, I felt the march was like an epic, it was a great epic for the entire group. And the *padre* said, "It's a shame," he said, "that we don't have a writer among us, someone to record something so epic, so wonderful. It's a shame we don't have a writer who could write and tell about the things we're doing." And that idea stayed with me.

• *Did you write something?*

Omar: No. The idea stuck, though, and came back to me later, in the mountains. And what had been epic for me then, as a child, was mundane in the mountains. But even though the marches were daily, there were epic moments. In terms of our growth, as human beings. Facing the elements, facing exhaustion, surviving. "Son of a bitch," I'd say to myself, "all this shit is going to be lost. No one's going to know about this." And I'll tell you something. I had my moments of feeling so tired, not exhausted exactly, but mentally tired, and I've had those moments since the mountains, as well. And even before going to the mountains. My last year at the university, I was spent, mentally. So in the mountains I had to find a kind of strength. Keep going. And I said to myself, "Son of a bitch, I probably won't be the one to do it, because I don't have the patience for writing." I didn't think *I* was going to write it. And, in effect, I didn't have the patience . . . really, I don't know why I was always thinking in terms of literature, because I'd never really read literature, just Cervantes, and that because I had to, because they made me, and it bored me. And later, *El Señor Presidente,* by Asturias. "But how great it would be," I'd say, "for someone to put all this down." I don't know why . . .

• *To communicate, maybe.*

Omar: No. It has more to do with Leonel. Because we had fun with a whole series of things, and years later I'd be thinking how he would have liked this or that. And I thought of literature in connection with him. I think it has something to do with Leonel.

• *So when you finally did decide to record your experiences, what was the process like?*

Omar: Look, love, I can't give the particulars, or the details. Enough to say that the way I recorded the book was pretty unorthodox and unconventional. It wasn't the way people generally write. Or maybe all writers write like that, and they just don't talk about it. Or maybe some do, and some don't. The most I can say is that in the book there are a good many unforgettable dawns, some *Flor de Caña* rum, rainy winter nights in which company and the verb come together . . . There are moments of spontaneous communication in the book. I never spent any time searching for the right word, or the best way to construct a sentence. That's why I say the method is pretty unorthodox and unconventional.

• *Okay, but you have your secretary . . . you're not going to tell me you didn't correct the transcription. Or someone else corrected it.*

Omar: Of course. I worked on it, and Sergio [Ramírez][5] helped me, but what I am trying to say . . . you don't understand.

• *Liliam[6] is important, too, in the making of the book. As important as the company you kept those rainy winter nights.*

Omar: Of course she is. That's why she's in the dedication.

• *And the next book? Do you think you're going to do a second volume? Because everyone's waiting . . .*

5. Sergio Ramirez, refer to Chapter One. He, and other writers and poets, helped Omar during the making of *The Mountain Is Something More than a Great Expanse of Green.*
6. Omar's secretary, who transcribed the tapes.

Omar: I think so, Margaret. What's happened is that we've been living a very tense situation here. And working very hard. So I haven't had the time to give myself the luxury of talking till dawn. There hasn't been the time to spend or to invest in that. I trust there'll come a time, in Nicaragua and throughout Central America, when we can go back to writing, and to so many other things.

• *Once you told me that Commander Borge gave you time off to do the book, a week off, in the country someplace.*

Omar: Near here, at Apoyo Lagoon. I taped for six hours, something like that. But I couldn't do any more.

• *Tell me a little about the book's reception. Not about the Casa de las Américas prize,*[7] *because you've already spoken about that, but about the people's reaction to the book, the common people of Nicaragua. Because the book is a real favorite among all kinds of people. Combatants love it.*

Omar: Look, Margaret, basically what the book has given me is a revolutionary satisfaction. After having been published and praised by so many people–and when I say so many, it's not a euphemism, it's real–I've had people come up to me, foreigners as well as Nicaraguans, and say, "You've changed my life with that book of yours!" Or, "Look, I want to tell you, your book helped us a lot in the neighborhood . . . in the jungle . . . in the base community." Or married couples, couples who have maybe had a fight and then make up with my book, and they come and tell me about it. Or revolutionary comrades, telling me that at difficult moments the book helped them get through. Even people from the bourgeoisie, who didn't understand the revolution but who came to understand it after reading my book.

• *That a revolutionary likes the book isn't hard to understand. But that a bourgeois person comes to understand the revolution through reading it seems very extraordinary to me.*

---

7. Omar's book won the Cuban prize in 1982.

Omar: Communists, too. A Colombian communist who didn't agree with the FSLN came around through reading the book. Just to give you an idea, I have more than a thousand letters. From the Canary Islands; from Belice; Mexico; Colombia; Panama; the United States; and from Open, kilometer 14 on the Juigalpa Highway; from Piedras Quemadas; Gancho de Camino–I mean from all over. I have more than a thousand letters. From all kinds of people: coffee cutters to reservists. *"Compa,"* they tell me, "we really love your book!" So, this book is a product of my need to love, right? And look how incredible: from this need of mine to love and be loved has come this, this thing that's dealt such a blow to imperialism!

• *And keeps engendering love among the people.*

Omar: And keeps engendering love. So, what can I say? To have participated as a guerrilla, to have written this book, son of a bitch: it's dealt a real blow to the enemy. You feel like you could die after something like that. After that book and one more. Or that book and two more. Or that book and five more. Or just that book. What I want to say is it's dealt a blow to im- perialism. I saw a photo, once, of a dead guerrilla in a Latin American country, and they showed everything he had in his knapsack: his plate, his spoon, his bedroll, his change of cloth- ing, and *The Mountain Is Something More than a Great Expanse of Green.* And I think back to when I was a guerrilla fighter; when a guerrilla carries a book in his knapsack, it really means some- thing. It's given me an incredible satisfaction. As a revolu- tionary, I'm happy because I think the book's dealt a blow to that son of a bitch, imperialism. How could I help from feeling satisfaction, for instance, when a Canadian comes and tells me they translated bits of the book and used them in their Sunday homilies at church? Or when someone tells me in three churches in Managua, on the altar–which is the most intimate part of the church–people have written excerpts from my book right there on the altar? That's a measure of influence and repercussion among the people.

• *Omar, your closest circles: your mama, your wife, and maybe your oldest daughter. Have they read the book? What do they think of it?*

Omar: My mama and Ruth, yes. My daughter, I don't think so.

- *What did your mama say?*

Omar: That it was very nice. That I tell it like it is. She knows the book was well thought of, she knows it's supposed to be a good book. Maybe she thinks it's good because her son's smart, eh? Something like that. As for Ruth, it's made her very happy. And she's grown to know me better through the book. Because at this point, Ruth is the person who knows me best, better than anyone else. She's pleased. But I think you should ask *her* what she thinks. It would be interesting, because I've never asked her directly.

- *Omar, do you like reading in public?*

Omar: I've only done it twice. I was a little nervous the first time because I was in a house full of intellectuals, right? And me, a commander, a military man, a political cadre for the FSLN. I felt a little strange. I'm used to standing up in front of people, and talking to them. But I felt strange because for the first time I was in front of people just to talk about myself. That's what made me nervous. I'm used to being in front of people, but not to talk about myself. Understand? I'm used to being in front of people to talk about the revolution, about others, but not about myself, not about me as a person. I've never been a personality.

- *But I think the secret of your book is that you talk about yourself, and the people—especially people here in Nicaragua, or in other places where there's struggle—people feel themselves and their experiences reflected in what you write. I remember the night that you read at the Fernando Gordillo Culture House, there were a lot of compas from the army there. You read about yourself, but everyone felt like you were talking about them.*

Omar: That's because I am the masses. That's the thing, Margaret. I am the masses. Even though I'm a cadre, I think like the masses. Sure, I'm a cadre because I work at a political level. But I think like the masses, I experience like the masses, I feel like the masses, and that's why I have this ability to communicate with the people. Because they're like me; because I'm like them. And I'm not the only one. If I didn't think like the masses, I'd have to make a big effort to reach the masses. But I talk to them the way I think, the way I feel. And they think and feel like me. That's the thing.

Contrition
(a fragment)

When Justo, two others, and I went exploring, looking for a contact with Modesto—who was surrounded by the Guard—Justo and I had been in the guerrilla together for about two years. I'd left Franklyn at the head of the rest of the group and I'd taken Justo with me because he inspired my confidence. Not just political confidence, but confidence in my ability to deal with the terrain and the problems we might have. With his help, with confidence in his fighting ability and in the fact that he wouldn't wander off on me after a battle. He was the lead guy, the first on all the marches, and I always walked right behind him, sure Justo wouldn't lose me on a fast retreat. Leave me alone? Think only of himself and forget about the others? Never! That was impossible with Justo. He really loved me. For Justo I was truth, victory. And he was such a noble guy, the most fraternal of them all. But he wasn't always fraternal. When Justo came up into the mountains with his brother, he came up with me. I was on my way back from a meeting with Bayardo Arce, in Estelí or Matagalpa. We came in a truck with four-wheel drive over a terrible mountain road going from Matagalpa to Cuá, and later we went on by foot, and Justo was real nervous. He was on his dark and rainy passage underground. When we got down from the truck and began to walk with the load we'd brought from the city, I didn't think I'd have any problems with these two guerrilla novices because they were country kids. Sons of a small or middle-level farmer. Young men raised between the farm and the townhouse. Between school and vacations working their family's rural property. When they'd grown some, I knew they had left school and gone to work with their father on his small farm. There was reason to believe, I thought, that these two wouldn't be prey to the repetitious tragicomedy of urban guerrillas who come into the mountains for the first time. But I was wrong. About an hour after we began our march, the moon our only light, and making our way up a difficult rise with little vegetation, Justo–the older of the two brothers, he was nineteen then–let his cargo drop, making noise near a house we were passing. His knapsack strap broke. Dogs barked at us, we could hear people moving about, a lamp went on inside the house and we had to crouch in the shadows so as not to be discovered. Justo was nervous, he knew he was responsible for what was going down. And although it wasn't the first time something like that had happened to me, I couldn't help but be irritated; situations like that endanger the whole guerrilla.

And that night it was the old tragicomedy all over again. Three hours out, and contrary to my predictions, Justo got dizzy. Then he vomited and finally, near dawn, after some six hours going up and down those hills looking for the camp at night, he passed out. We had to let him sleep it off, and stay the day in some thick bush. The next day Justo woke shamefaced and doubly upset. He was upset because his younger brother had come off better than he had, and he was upset because he knew I was the guerrilla chief. He knew who I was; he knew I was Juan José. When I looked at him, he lowered his eyes and I'd look him over without seeming to, trying to figure him out. Check his way of moving, his physical presence, his habits, his facial expressions. You learn about people that way.

Justo was taller than me. About five foot ten. He had an oval face, though it filled out when there was enough to eat, and he'd put some weight on. When there wasn't much, he had an oval face. His lips were fine, his teeth even. He had a few false teeth, but not gold ones; white ones. His eyes were brown, his hair straight and he parted it down the middle. Justo came lean to the guerrilla and he was kind of pale, a little stooped. But with time he got stronger and his face was less drawn. Though he always had a small, kind of pointed chin. He had a big nose, a nose like Dante Alighieri's. And then, in time, he was no longer lean or stooped. He was never very muscular, but I'd say he was full of body and had real strong legs.

In time, with me goading him all the way, Justo changed his manner of walking, the way he was. Because at the beginning he was kind of spoiled, but I'd get on him and I'd tell him, "Comrade, leave that kind of thing to the Guard." And when he'd retreat into that way he had, I'd try to make him feel bad. I'd criticize him and say, "We'll see if that's how you're gonna talk to the enemy, when the time comes!"

I really worked on Justo's individual combat development. And on his political and human formation. I paid a lot of personal attention to him, especially after I realized he could find his way through those mountains. Someone who could find his way in those mountains, then, was worth ten who couldn't. And so I took him on, didn't let anything go by; nothing. I was always on top of him. And I could see the kid assimilated. He learned everything. Soon I realized he was a potential cadre; all I had to do was be tough and consistent and he'd grow. Not let him get away with anything. Justo was like a blotter; he just absorbed things out of the air. There weren't many of us at that time, and I was beginning to see that Justo could become my second-in-command; and that made me hit even harder at him, not let him get away with anything. And I know there were times I went too far! He was hard on me, too, and since I was the chief, the guy was always observing me: what I did, how I did it, why I did it. And if I was doing what I made him do. I had to do it all, too, and better than he.

Justo's personality changed little by little. Now he was neither stooped nor thin. He grew into a strong military man. And a military man with a deep political consciousness, a knowledge of why he was doing what he was doing. He always wore his cap proper and clean, and he didn't like anyone to poke or pull at it. When we camped and it got wet, he dried it right away. I never saw his belt buckle that it wasn't squarely over the waistband of his pants.

Justo developed fast. He learned all the old-timer's ways, the good ones and the bad. He even learned to dream watching the campfire go out, when everyone else was asleep and only he and I were still up cooking some monkey and listening to Radio Havana. He learned to look the comrades in the eye. He learned to walk and to haul and he even became a bit proud and sure of himself; still humble, though, because Justo was the humblest of them all. He learned to be intransigent with himself and with the rest, and he learned to love me when I criticized him for not being on top of things, for being too sure of himself or too comfortable. He learned to love me through sleeping two years with me in the same hammock. He learned to love me through a thousand nights together talking about the immortality of the crab, the reproduction of ants, springtime and far-off lands, Modesto and Claudia, believing me wise when I'd tell him of dialectical materialism and of historical materialism, and singing Mexican *rancheras* together in the middle of the jungle until we stopped and the next day dawned without even realizing we'd slept.

He learned to love me till he was willing to give his life
for me or give me the best of whatever it was we had, or
the prettiest. Just because he loved me, and not because
I was the chief. What he never understood was that I
began to love him too, that he became a part of me.
What he never knew was that every day I trusted him
more. Every day I placed more hope and faith in him.
That I dug him, the way he was. That each day that
passed I trusted him more and that his being there gave
me more confidence in my own ability; as he learned to
know the moons, to know and understand the sounds
of the wind. As he became the most disciplined of them
all and could handle a machete as well as the international or national news. As he lived more and more
according to the toughest security measures, became
more and more concerned with the guerrilla's life and
its future. Justo was all tenderness in his eyes when he
shouted out warnings and criticisms or words of encour-
agement to the other comrades.

Justo felt safe with me, but he never knew that, in time,
it became a reciprocal thing. He couldn't have known
that, by then, I was willing to give my life for his. He
couldn't have imagined that his company gave me
confidence and lucidity; he couldn't know that beside
him I felt protected. He didn't suspect that beside him I
was more fearless. He didn't know I loved him. I'd
never thought it prudent to tell him so. I was the chief,
and for ethical—or political, or military—reasons I hesi-
tated telling a subordinate that I, his leader, felt safe and
protected in his company.

I never told him—least of all then, surrounded as we
were by the Guard, on the verge of unequal battle to
save our lives, which at that particular moment hung
from a thread.

1983

Gioconda Belli

Deciding to make my work the best poem I could write

"Now, when there's been so much debate here about the role of
the writer in the revolution, I've given it a lot of thought, and
I've come to some conclusions. In the first place, of course, it's
up to each individual what he or she decides to do. And that
depends a great deal on the person's unique development and
also on his or her place within the revolutionary process. Today
there are tasks in this revolution which demand all our energy.
Not as writers, but as organizers. And while it's true that art,
creativity, has its social function and is important in the revolutionary context, it's no less true that there are priorities. In my
case, the task assigned me demands a great deal of creative
energy, much dedication and time; all I have, really. And all this
has led me to decide to try to make my work the best poem I
could write."

It's Gioconda Belli speaking. By the time we finally sit down
to talk, it's already late at night. Gioconda carries an important
work load and responsibility in the area of the revolution's
information service—getting the truth out, in a world of calcu-
lated misinformation—and it's not easy for her to find time or
space in which to speak of her own life and work. Yet her poetry
has been important, even outside Nicaragua, from the time of
her 1978 Casa de las Américas award (for her book *Línea de*

frente—Front Line), and I begin by asking her to go deeper into this whole question of the dilemma faced by the revolutionary writer in a time of such intense struggle.

Gioconda: We artists must become conscious of the fact that our work, although created individually, comes out of a social practice. In this sense, at least in my opinion, the most important thing is being able to assume and to sustain a social practice that's truly—objectively—satisfying. A concrete activity which, through its own dynamic, will lead to our personal transformation. In today's Nicaragua, this immerses us in the tasks of a people who are struggling to eradicate the past and build the future.

As poets, there's another level to this, as well. We must get rid of those characteristics which have made us "conflictive" or "difficult" in the past. So that one day we will stop hearing people excuse us or brush us off with the comment, "Oh . . . he's a poet!" said with scorn, as if to say, "What can you expect?" And that's not a gratuitous saying. It's been earned to a certain extent, although it's certainly also often exaggerated. It's something that's come out of our own social development. And so we must understand and accept the fact that for us artists the process of maturity, of internal revolution, may perhaps be more difficult than for others. We must discipline ourselves, take a strong stand against our weaknesses, and work for the respect our real contribution to society can bring us.

And it's not only up to us to decide what our contribution to society should be. It depends on the needs of the process. It's a difficult decision because sometimes one thinks one could be writing good and useful things, developing one's work, which also has its social function. But, in my particular case, I've decided to devote myself to my work—at least for a time. I believe that this will help me transform myself as a human being, and at the same time, when it becomes possible, will allow me to create an art with more integrity.

Oh, I don't mean that I won't write a poem if I feel the need. But I believe that my role in the revolution, at least at this point in time, is to do my work as well as I can. And that's what I plan on giving my energies to, for now.

• *What you're saying is very interesting, Gioconda. But I'd like you to try to go deeper into the process that led you to this decision.*

Gioconda: It probably has a lot to do with my personal history. I came to political militancy and to poetry at more or less the same time in my life. But the former was always more important to me than the latter. I clearly remember a poem by Francisco de Asís Fernández, a poem he wrote in the seventies, in which he said "we won't bring the dictatorship and injustice down by poems alone." I always believed that intellectual work was important, but that what really counted was concrete action, concrete and practical personal commitment. And I still believe that. Because we're still at war. But I repeat: I'm just speaking out of my personal experience. Because I am sure there are other *compañeros* who will decide to dedicate themselves to their writing and, through that, give a great deal to the revolution as well. One is as legitimate as the other. It depends on the individual.

• *Gioconda, tell me about your life.*

Gioconda: Well, I've had a very fortunate life. And I think my greatest fortune lies in having been able to be a part of the Sandinista National Liberation Front since 1970. I was recruited by Camilo Ortega. If that hadn't happened, I really can't imagine what my life would have become. Because I was born into a well-to-do family in Nicaraguan "high society." And that gave me a great many privileges. I studied in Europe and in the United States, where I specialized in advertising and journalism. When I was eighteen, I married "well." And I guess I really did marry "well" because I have two beautiful daughters from that union. But there came a time when I began feeling an intense contradiction between the life I was leading and what I saw going on around me. I noticed these contradictions first of all because my Christian upbringing made such great injustice intolerable to me, and secondly because my family were traditional Conservatives and anti-Somoza. And I grew up in an atmosphere of opposition to the regime. But I could never see a way out. I didn't know what I might do. All I knew was that I couldn't go on living the kind of life I was living.

In 1969, I was lucky enough to meet a group of *compañeros* who began explaining a few things to me. They began raising my consciousness little by little, and introducing me to a few simple tasks I might do. And then I made contact with Camilo in 1970 and began collaborating with the FSLN. I was more frightened than anything else, to tell the truth! But what happened? That whole process of discovering a meaning to my life, meeting a different kind of person, also motivated my beginning to write. So the two came hand in hand, you might say. And I began to write. I wrote out of all the euphoria I felt at being alive, at being a woman, a mother—it was a deeply erotic poetry, in the broadest sense of that term. Not only in the sexual sense to which it's often limited. I was singing out of my pleasure at being alive, of feeling glad to be a woman and living in a time when things were happening which promised such important changes.

I also was rebelling against the hypocrisy of society. Because at first I spoke very innocently of the things I was feeling, I saw nothing wrong with talking about my body or about such beautiful and daily things as making love. Men had been writing about those things for centuries. But it became scandalous that a well-bred girl from the Asunción—as Beltrán would say— would use words like belly, breast, and so on. Or say she wanted to run naked through the hills . . . that a *woman* would dare speak in that way of her body, of her sensuality. When I began to feel the effects of the scandal and heard the commentaries being made, I realized I had encroached upon one of society's "sacred areas," where it was "immoral" to speak of physical love. But poverty, prostitution, and crime were not immoral. Those who were so scandalized by what I was writing felt quite at home with all that.

I intuitively understood that what I was doing was rebelling. Coronel Urtecho once said that the woman who reveals herself rebels. And I kept it up, although it cost me the disapproval of many . . . even people close to me, in my own family. I had to put up with a sort of myth which was created about me, as if I were the only woman in the world who felt those things that all normal, healthy women feel.

A lot of people tell me how brave I am to write these things. That always seems strange to me because they are things that practically everyone has the "courage" to feel. And to do. Besides, love is a very beautiful thing. And the human being is not simply a spirit, but expresses his or her love through the body. So what has to do with the body should not produce that kind of shame. That's simply primitive hypocrisy, the product of a hypocritical and deformed society.

Of course, that experience also helped me realize that rebellion was the way. And that the revolution was primary: the dream we had to make reality, the most urgent poem all Nicaraguans had to help write in order that we could begin building a more just society; in order to be able to create the material basis, the new relations of production, which will allow a new man and a new woman to come into being.

So I threw myself wholeheartedly into political commitment, and I was lucky to be able to work with comrades who taught me so many things, who helped me grow. It was a difficult process for me, in many ways, because I had to break with a whole way of life, with a whole series of values which had been inculcated in me. I'm still breaking with them. But it was through that whole process of pain and joy that I found the way to my integral development as a human being, as a social being who can only change herself insofar as she actively participates in changing society.

• *Thinking back on your early political activity and your emerging craft as a poet, how did you move between one and the other? Did they stimulate one another, or were there conflicts there?*

Gioconda: Well, there was a period when, because of the particular kind of work I was involved in, the FSLN advised me to be careful not to "burn" myself. I had to make sure I didn't publish anything that might reveal my true political feelings. After the 1972 earthquake, Somoza's security police got wise to me and I began to be followed. At that time I was working as a messenger between René Núñez and Eduardo Contreras.[1] The people where I worked at that time told me that the head of Somoza's security force had told them to fire me because I belonged to the FSLN. I didn't let on there was anything wrong, and I remember that my poetry was a useful cover with them, because that was how I justified my hanging around with a few "strange" people, as they called them.

The day after they gave me that little message from Samuel Genie,[2] I noticed that there was a jeep always following me. It really scared me when I realized that. I had already separated from my husband, and I was living alone with my two daughters. I managed to contact the *compañeros*, and they instructed me to "cool off," as we said in those days. I was afraid, until I realized that was exactly what they were trying to do to me—make me afraid, intimidate me so I'd break down and quit. After that, what I felt was mostly a tremendous rage and hatred for them. And breaking down was the last thing I would have done, especially as it was just about that time that I received a letter telling me I'd been accepted as a militant in the Front. That was a great stimulus for me.

But of course the fact I was being followed meant I was already "burnt." I lay low, and they stopped following me after a few months. When I "thawed out" I went back to work at various tasks, one of them being one of the support teams created for the December 27th 1974 action.[3] Before that action the comrades told me to leave the country, because they were expecting repression against everyone who was involved. So I left for two months, but then came back for another year—until my immediate superior was taken prisoner, and again I was ordered out of the country.

1. René Núñez is the Secretary of the FSLN's National Directorate today. Eduardo Contreras, leader of the organization, was killed in 1976.

2. Samuel Genie was Somoza's Chief of Security Police.

3. On December 27, 1974, an FSLN commando occupied the home of a Somoza superior when a Christmas party was in session. Many high-level hostages were taken, and the organization obtained the release of all the political prisoners, a million dollars, and publication of two communiqués important to the Nicaraguan people.

All those years I was writing and publishing, and my being a poet enabled me to move in diverse circles where I could obtain information. My book *Sobre la grama [On the Grass]*, which won the "Mariano Fiallos Gil" poetry prize from the National University, is from those years. The only conflict I had was making sure I didn't publish anything that would give my real sentiments away. That's why *Sobre la grama* is not a book of political poetry as such, although it is certainly a book that deals with society's hypocrisy toward women.

• *But* Línea del fuego, *the book that won the Casa de las Américas poetry prize and really made your name outside the country, is an eminently political book.*

Gioconda: But by then we were already beginning another stage. I wrote *Línea de fuego* during the first four months of my exile in Mexico. I was ordered to leave the country as a preventive measure, but I had the hope of being able to return. But later my name was mentioned publicly, I was condemned *in absentia* by a court-martial, and logically it wasn't just me who had been burned, but a large part of the work of the FSLN outside the country was exposing what was happening in Nicaragua. So everything I'd been accumulating throughout those years, my deepest feelings, the pain of the repression we had suffered, exile, the separation from my children—all this came out in my poetry, poured out in that book which I finished—along with a few other poems—in 1977.

• *What was it like for you to receive the coveted Casa de las Américas prize?*

Gioconda: It was a great stimulus, of course. And especially at just that point in time, when the struggle was escalating. And it enabled me to travel a lot and to speak about Nicaragua. It helped me in my work outside the country because the prize carries a great deal of intellectual prestige; it opens doors, and we needed every door open to tell the world what was happening in our country. I also understood that I was learning how to communicate things, to sensitize people about what we Nicaraguans were going through. So I understood that being a poet could also be a weapon in the struggle, and that it was my responsibility to attain a level of quality which would allow me to motivate people, get my message across. I was also happy because that book is a mixture of love and revolution, and I saw that it was possible to write love poems which were also revolutionary, which could integrate personal and collective experiences.

At first I had problems with the so-called political poems. They always came out of my own individual experiences, and I considered that to be a limitation. But when one lives collective experiences as an individual—although the form appears to be personal, or one speaks in the first person—the truth is that one expresses feelings or ideas which have the force of many experiences born from collective practice and struggle. And that's what gives them a political value.

• *Your poetry after July 19th [1979] has always seemed to me to be very different from your poetry before the victory, although one is certainly a logical progression from the other. What has it been like for you, being a poet in this period of victory and relative peace?*

Gioconda: Well, exile dried me up as a poet. I went for a long time without writing anything because I needed my roots: the lakes, the volcanoes, the heat, the faces of the people, the smells, the clouds. When I returned to Nicaragua—you can imagine how marvelous, how fantastic it was to see the reality one had dreamed of for so long, for which so many people had given their lives, so many beloved friends . . . to know that those deaths, all that suffering had not been in vain. It was an incredible sensation of strength, of security. You realize that dreams are possible. I still get goose bumps in the demonstrations, seeing the masses of red and black flags, listening to the Sandinista anthem sung by thousands of voices. At first it all seemed too good to be true. Then, after recovering my roots, after several months of such profound emotions, I began to write again.

The first poem was about July 19th, what I felt that day. Then I took up poetry again and, of course, time doesn't pass in vain. There's an error in the introduction to the book I published after the victory, *Truenos y arcoiris [Thunder and Rainbow]*. It says that all those poems are from the year before and two years after the victory. That's not true. They are all written after the triumph. There was a process of poetic maturation; more craft, more rigor. It reflects a whole process of internal confrontation with dream becoming reality, but which I think still needs building, polishing.

And it's also a process of internal revolution, which becomes more intense during peacetime–even during this relative peace–because it's a search for the revolution on other levels, deeper levels. The revolution from the inside out, the search for one's authentic identity, for new human relations which are difficult because one knows that it's necessary to destroy much of the past, but we don't really know what we're going to replace it with. I'm talking about the more intimate level; the traditional man-woman relationships, for example.

That whole process can really hurt. Because sometimes I think it's easier to face an enemy army in combat than to confront the inheritance of concepts and prejudices we carry inside ourselves and to transform it. It's tremendously difficult for all of us. It produces enormous contradictions, and we don't have any models at hand because it's something new that has to be created. So those are the thunderclaps, the thunder: those blows from our own inexperience. But then there's always the rainbow, the hope, the collective transformation that's taking place and that we are part of. The beautiful experiences, the volcanic energy of this people, which gives us new lessons every day. This people, of whom we are a part.

With all this change, it's only logical that my poetry would be something different after the victory. And I feel an even greater responsibility to write the best poetry I can, to make sure it communicates, is useful, that it transcends. For example, even though it's not my best poem–in a literary sense–"No pasarán" ["They Shall Not Pass"], which Carlos Mejía Godoy put to music, is for me the most important poem I've written since the triumph. I feel that so many people have been moved by what it says. And that's been an enormously satisfying experience for me.

When I go back to being a poet (because I mentioned earlier that I'm going to "retire" for a while), I think I'll learn to play the guitar so I can sing my poems. One of my dreams is to be able to sing; I'm a frustrated singer. And as they say, it's not necessarily the great voice that counts, but the feeling behind it—well, it might work. But, all joking aside, as long as Nicaragua continues to suffer this situation of daily aggression, which the Reagan administration's belligerent irresponsibility inflicts upon us, I think that the artist's slogan will have to go on being what Fernando Gordillo always said: "Struggle is the highest form of song."

• *I agree with that, Gioconda, but the fact is that a poet always writes poetry, even when prevented by circumstances from giving his or her full attention to writing poems. I'd like you to try to go into the present situation in more detail, look at the current situation of psychological warfare (apart from its other manifestations) and its impact on the writer, the poet, in his or her specifically creative sphere.*

Gioconda: It's hard for me to answer that kind of question just now, because we're in such a difficult situation. There's such a great daily tension, the danger of war all the time. One feels sad because one realizes that all of this which has been constructed with such love, with so much enthusiasm and hope, can be destroyed at any time by the irrationality of a system incapable of accepting the fact that there are people who are not willing to do its divine will. A system that believes that the destiny of the Americas is its to decide, and that that destiny does not belong to the people who live it. So when one sees such beautiful things in the revolution, like the other day when I wrote a poem after a long time of not writing anything, it's very painful.

I was with my older daughter, in the Plaza. They were commemorating the death of Carlos Fonseca, and at that commemoration many young people, including her, were being initiated into the Sandinista Youth Movement. And I saw that Plaza filled with people, beautiful faces, laughing young people: that joy, that enthusiasm, that revolutionary fervor. And I got to thinking that all that could simply be destroyed. Just like that. Of course, when I say "destroyed" I don't really mean that completely. Because on a certain level I believe that what we've built is indestructible. Even if they killed the last Nicaraguan, we would have made a lasting contribution to history and to humanity.

But a few days after that commemoration in the Plaza, I wrote a poem about that moment. It's about one's sense of continuity, in a way. Thinking that the things, the thoughts, all that we do is transcendent when we do it with love, when it's revolution. And that my daughter was in some way a prolongation or continuation of a road I chose: the revolution which she is also choosing now as she enters the Youth Movement. It seemed to me that at that moment I gave birth to her. Because it's easy to bear a child—physically speaking—but it's not so easy to give birth to a child's consciousness. And the greatest satisfaction one can feel is seeing that consciousness being born, that commitment and devotion to the things one loves most.

I think our youth are our revolution's greatest accomplishment. And they are acquiring that consciousness. It's a consciousness of values which are no longer individualistic and egoistic. They are not of the same society in which we were raised. They are learning collective values, full of love, full of poetry. Young people here, all our people, are writing one big collective poem.

And this is really a country of poets. Our people are constantly carrying out acts of poetry. Yesterday, speaking with a journalist, I thought of a *compañero*, a combatant, who told me something he did in the middle of a battle: the counterrevolution was attacking his town, and he worked in a movie house. In the small towns the theaters put loudspeakers in the streets to call people to see the show. So he went to his theater, he made his way through the cross fire, and put some revolutionary music on full blast to raise the spirit of the combatants. That's such a beautiful thing to me. I don't know if things like that happen in other places.

• *To finish up, Gioconda, would you like to talk a bit about your life within the revolution, not only from the point of view of a poet, but from the point of view of a woman? I know that you do a lot of think-*

*ing about your condition as a woman within the revolutionary proc-
ess. What conclusions have you reached?*

Gioconda: I think this revolution has made women grow in a
direction for which quite possibly we are not yet prepared. I
don't say my situation is typical. Because I had a social status
and educational level not common in our country. So I'm not
going to speak about the problem of women in general, but
about professional women, working women, who aren't necessarily part of the elite, but who are the majority of women who
work, who have gained a certain consciousness of themselves
both as women and as social beings.

On our jobs, in our work places, we have achieved a considerable level of equality, I believe, in comparison with other Latin
American countries and even in comparison with most European countries—as far as I could see on a recent trip, when I had
the opportunity of speaking with women from several feminist
organizations. Here women have a level of social involvement
won during the war. We have equal opportunities, and our
opinions are taken into consideration. But this has made us live
"like men." We have taken on a series of responsibilities which
has given us a life which corresponds more to the pattern of life
which has traditionally been the realm of men in our society.

So this has left us with a great many unresolved aspects, still.
The whole emotional part. Because while, on the one hand,
professional women are recognized and stimulated in their
work—and I think there's a great deal of liberation in Nicaragua
in this respect—on the emotional side, a great many old patterns
are maintained. The woman who has won her place in society—
in ways in which only men did previously—now lives like a
man, but alone. Because what happens? The ordinary man sees
her as an "equal" and therefore not as a woman. Because his
idea of a woman is not yet that of "equal." A woman for most
men here is still someone who is submissive, who stays home,
who behaves in a completely traditional way. So a woman who
has freed herself in this way may have excellent men friends,
close relationships, *compañeros* who tell her their troubles, who
confide in her, and who share many things with her, but never

occurs to think of her as a possible companion. The minute that idea comes up, they begin to back off. They can't deal with it.

This has nothing to do with a party line. In fact, the FSLN's line regarding this situation is just the opposite. The party encourages equality in all aspects of human relationships. But it's a problem the men themselves have. Many of them have yet to move forward in this respect. I've spoken to many of the *compañeros* about this problem. And they realize it's a problem, they understand that it's a manifestation of *machismo*, of their own insecurity. But they don't yet know how to deal with it, really. They don't yet know how to overcome their fear of a woman who is their "equal." *Who is their equal, but a woman.* So the revolution has given us many things, but on the plane of emotional relationships between men and women there are still unresolved problems. *We women must remain in the vanguard around this.*

I demand people accept me as a poet

As a small child, Daisy Zamora was shy and sometimes remote, and as a woman she continues to be seen by many as reserved. She is a person who listens more than she speaks. As someone with strong revolutionary convictions—and history—she nevertheless retains the image of a middle-class woman concerned with appearances and manners. One doesn't expect to see Daisy without the appropriate dress or outside the context of a certain subtle elegance.

Those who know this enigmatic woman see beneath that. She comes from a well-to-do family, a family of Liberals, in which bourgeois politics became the nightly dinner conversation. Her father participated in the 1954 movement against the elder Somoza, and he was discovered and imprisoned because of it. (Daisy was four then; she was told that he was on a business trip, but she recognized his picture on the front page of the daily paper. Faced by her family's refusal to admit she was right—that it was really his face she saw—she suffered with nightmares for years.)

Daisy wasn't raised by her parents but by a great-aunt and a grandfather who would be a decisive force in her life. She studied at the convent schools that were typical of her class and culture; she read constantly, and to a large extent she found refuge in books. Later, studying psychology at the university, she met Dionisio Marenco, who would become her husband. Together, they explored political questions which—in her case—had their roots in the social concerns of her childhood. With Nicho, Daisy joined the student movement already led by the FSLN in the late sixties. Later on, she went with Nicho to a sugar plantation in the department of Chinandega, where their life as revolutionaries began in earnest.

Nicho and Daisy were part of the urban support structure for the attack on the National Palace, in August 1978. Half of the commando hid in her house to make its final preparations. Daisy herself finally took part in urban combat, and toward the end of the war, she was one of the voices heard over the underground "Radio Sandino." Since the victory, she has been Vice-Minister of Culture, part of a team studying religion in postwar Nicaragua, director of the North American desk at the FSLN's Department of International Relations, and currently she heads the publishing program at a research institute.

Our conversation took place at Daisy's home, a house in Managua to which she and Nicho had recently moved. The hall and living room were still almost empty; only a beautiful collection of Nicaraguan paintings and a bicycle—Daisy's—met my eye. We settled on a veranda facing the inner garden, and began talking.

• *Daisy, what does it mean to you to be a poet? What does it contribute to or take from your life?*

Daisy: That's a difficult question, isn't it?

• *But you feel like a poet, don't you?*

Daisy: I think being a poet is a way of looking at life. It's not something you can choose to be or not to be. You simply *are.* Am I making sense? Sometimes when I read a statement by one or another of the comrades, even your own interviews, and they speak of that dilemma between the craft and one's revolutionary responsibility . . . I've really never felt that contradiction that seems so difficult to others. Because I think you are a

poet whether or not you are able to write, at a given moment.
It's the way you see and feel things.

   A while back, I was thinking of writing a series of poems and
I was reading E.E. Cummings for inspiration. And I came across
a phrase of his in the introduction to one of his books: "poetry
is; it isn't made." I totally agree with that.

For me there is no contradiction between being a poet and being a revolutionary. All we have to do is look at poets like Leonel Rugama. It certainly wasn't a contradiction for Leonel. He lived his poetry; you read his work, and it's his life. He was simply consistent, that's all. And I think all poets must be consistent, true to their work. We can't all be Leonel Rugama. But think of someone like Ernesto Mejía Sánchez, another poet important to us all. He's one of our great voices; he's not aggressive politically, but Mejía Sánchez's life is just as consistent with his work as Leonel's was, and he plays an important role in Nicaraguan literature. And consequently, an important role in our revolution.

So when I read page after page about whether or not one can be a poet and also a revolutionary, about the so-called contradiction between the two conditions, it really bothers me. Because, for me, it's always been clear. There's nothing complicated about it. One must be faithful to one's poetic being, and as I said before, it's a condition, not something you can acquire.

As for what being a poet gives me or takes away, there are things that condition one's life, make you particularly sensitive to certain things and give you the possibility of expressing them—which is really what it is, perhaps, to be a poet. I think that's what you're asking me.

In my case, my childhood, the experiences from those years, have been decisive. Everything which was a part of the world I lived in then, experiences and images, conditioned me to see the world in a certain way. And I think that's clear in my verse. It's something I hold onto, it's something that makes me feel good. If one is able to capture what Pound called the image, if you can really say it out, if you manage to make your internal experience coincide with a certain form of expression in time—a valid expression—when you achieve that, you feel enormously satisfied. I think that's the great advantage of being a poet.

The disadvantage is that there's no getting away from it. And, although at times you'd like another logic in your life, you come to realize that despite everything you always react in a particular way . . . and that if you lose that, you simply stop being a poet. You stop seeing life through a poet's eyes.

• *I agree, Daisy, that one* is *a poet. That it's not something one becomes. Now, how does your being a poet–something that deep, that integral–affect the other conditions of your life: you as a woman comrade, mother, revolutionary, friend, worker?*

Daisy: Look, as long as one keeps on growing, in the true sense of the word, one gradually becomes clearer and clearer about one's priorities. About those things to which you must give preference. Because that's what helps you move forward, qualitatively, as a human being. About ten years ago–although I had become conscious of the fact that I see things differently from other people, and I was able to express those things in a way that others could share; although I was conscious even then of having this special condition, of *being a poet*–I now realize I also had less of what we might call the vital consciousness necessary to really exercise the craft. That is, I had not been sufficiently aware of the importance–for me–of really living as a poet. Of demanding to be accepted as one. Of making my condition take root and of being in harmony with that condition, even though it might create difficulties in the other areas of my life.

Ten years back I wasn't conscious enough of this. Now I'd like to nurture this awareness because I've made too many concessions. I've tried to adapt myself to others–without losing that other part of me but never demanding real respect for it, never really challenging the rest of the world. Not necessarily in an aggressive way, but so they would accept me as a poet, as I am.

This consciousness has deepened in me as the years pass. As you accumulate experiences, those experiences themselves make things come clearer for you. You begin to see the things with which you truly identify, and what you're capable of doing. After all these years, I've arrived at the point where I demand people accept me as a poet. Even if this may bring me problems I find difficult to face . . . in the family, as well as at the social, and even political levels.

• *What kind of political problems?*

Daisy: Well, I think there are difficult moments in the very development of the revolution, in the development of the organizational structures being created, and the sensibility or radar—if you will—that one has, as a poet, for capturing and reproducing what's important in life. That radar causes me problems at times. Because it's turned on even when I don't necessarily want it to be. I'm in a formative stage, I'm trying to learn from the revolution, and there are times the hypersensitivity can get in your way.

Always having this extreme sensitivity is a problem when one has to confront situations which, as a revolutionary conscious of the overall process, you must master. This is the kind of thing I've been going through. I don't know if other poets have this kind of experience. It's not really that it's an obstacle, but I think I have a slight disadvantage, compared to others.

• *It seems to me, that as the revolutionary process itself develops and matures, what may be a disadvantage today may become an advantage later on.*

Daisy: Of course. I'm talking about right now. I know that in the future, as the revolution consolidates itself and things become better organized, it's going to be a great advantage. It will be more and more important to be able to be sensitive to everything, to always have your radar turned on. But sometimes I think of [Vladimir] Mayakovsky. He killed himself because of a series of problems which were perfectly soluble, seen in an objective way. But he himself said, in this last letter: "The ship of love was shattered by everyday life." Later, one of the revolutionary leaders, who was also a writer, wrote a very good analysis of the reasons for Mayakovsky's suicide, and called him the best poet of the revolution, up to that time. Or rather, representative of the best of Russian literary tradition to that point. I'm giving you a very dramatic and extreme example, to illustrate my belief that in a transitional process you must take into account that some of us poets are somewhat more vulnerable than the average person. It's not a question of capacity, but of condition. Of conditioning, if you like . . .

• *I'm reminded of Haydeé Santamaría. She wasn't a poet in the sense Mayakovsky was, of course, but certainly in the broadest—and deepest—sense of that word she was very much a poet. She had a poet's soul, a spirit so exquisitely tuned; she was able to give so very much to the Cuban revolutionary process . . . yet in the end she couldn't go on living. Daisy, are you writing much poetry these days?*

Daisy: Well, I have a lot of notes. Things I haven't had time to work on. My job load has been really heavy. Right now I feel I need some space in order to polish what I have. I also feel the need to publish a second book. Not for the sake of its publication, but in order to be able to see another stage of work concretized. In order to begin something new. Am I making sense? My first book is a selection from ten years of work,[1] and it's already somehow far from me. I feel I'm someone else, now, to a great extent.

• *Do you have new poems now, that are already something else?*

Daisy: Yes. I had set November as my goal for having the new book ready, but now I don't think I'll make it because I haven't been able to get the time I need for it. But I think perhaps in a few months more . . . not in November, but later on, I'll get the book out.

• *What are your new poems about?*

Daisy: Well, some are about people in the revolution; there's one about a news vendor, another about a waitress, another about a coconut seller: images of people in the street, people I see on my way to and from work, each one with a certain significance. They seem to explain the reality I see around me every day. That's one of the themes in the new poems. And the rest are in the same vein as before, but from a different perspective.

• *Does the book have a name yet?*

Daisy: Are you kidding? What I have are a few finished poems and others still in draft form that I haven't even been able to get back to. It really worries me, because I'm always thinking about

---

1. *La violenta espuma [The Violent Foam],* poems 1968–1978, Ministry of Culture, Managua, Nicaragua. 1981.

them, I'm constantly thinking I must finish them. Sometimes you leave a poem too long and it dies on you. At least that's what happens to me. Sometimes I lose the momentum or the experience itself. And I begin to see it as alien, I can't keep working on it and then I've lost it. I've aborted several poems that way.

• *Daisy, at the beginning of this interview you mentioned two American poets. First, e.e. cummings, and then Ezra Pound. I know American poetry has had a great deal of influence in Nicaragua, above all because of the work of José Coronel Urtecho and Ernesto Cardenal, through the anthology they edited. Has American poetry been especially important to you, to your own work?*

Daisy: Of course. I've never denied I'm the daughter of Coronel and of Cardenal. Just as I'm the child of modernism, of Darío, as we all are. I also think the vanguard generation made a decisive contribution to the poets of my generation. And now there's this whole movement of poetry workshops—which is something else again—and we're really not the "younger" generation anymore.

I could never deny that North American poetry has been important to me. In Coronel's and Cardenal's translations, we began to read Ezra Pound, Walt Whitman, George Oppen, Cummings, Carl Sandburg, William Carlos Williams, Emily Dickinson. On the other hand, I studied at a bilingual school, where we read English and North American literature as a matter of course. That's where I discovered the English romantic poets; as a child I remember reading Keats, Shelley, Elizabeth Barrett Browning, Byron, and others. Those poets were familiar to me. They were a part of my education.

There's one North American poet who influenced me a great deal, and I don't even know to what extent she may have been crucial to me; that's Emily Dickinson. I read her a lot as a young girl. I was a shy, romantic, and withdrawn child, and I was impressed and fascinated by the life of this woman no one even knew was a poet, a mysterious woman from Amherst, Massachusetts, whose work no one knew until after her death. I read her poetry in English because there weren't any translations;

just the occasional version of a single poem. Recently a friend gave me the Visor anthology—bilingual. Yes, I think North American poetry has been very important to me. I love those poets, and I owe them all a great debt.

• *And which Nicaraguan poets particularly interest you, Daisy?*

Daisy: Well, I have my preferences in poetry as I do in everything else. Personal preferences. I'd say my favorite Nicaraguan poets are Joaquín Pasos, Alfonso Cortés, and Coronel—my relationship with Coronel is a filial one; I look on him as a father and a teacher—and, of course, Ernesto [Cardenal]. This doesn't mean I don't also enjoy the poetry of Pablo Antonio Cuadra, of Angel Martínez, Azarías Pallais, Ernesto Mejía Sánchez—he's certainly one of our great poets—and Carlos Martínez Rivas. Martínez Rivas is really especially important to me. I think he's one of our greatest poets, and I read his poems as often as I can.

Oh, and I remember the name of another North American poet now: Amy Lowell. She's one I left out; and Carl Sandburg. I even have a poem about a waitress, nothing like Sandburg's poems about a waitress, but inevitably the same thing that moved him to write about that woman, who he felt was different from the rest, moved me to write a poem totally different from his, but about the same kind of character. I read his poem years ago, and sometimes I think a lot about association, to what extent can a poem read many years ago awake in you the capacity to perceive something which might have otherwise gone unnoticed . . .

The Waitress

From table to table
she gathers the empty beer bottles,
piles the plates on a plastic tray
and her thick fingers like claws
raise five glasses clicking together.

Like a fat comet she travels her orbit:
the work heats her face
makes her arms tremble, and the small breasts
beneath the blue dress
with apron tied about her hips.

She goes from table to table
until the talk thins
the kitchen noises cease
and the customers disperse.
Buses stop
and the moon is high
above the street lamps.

Closing
she places the chairs on the tables
and slumps in the back of the restaurant.
Straining, she removes her shoes,
puts her feet up on a stool
and turns out her apron pockets
to count
one by one
the day's coins.

I think that what's so marvelous about poetry, it makes you pay attention, it awakens you to to things you might never notice, it gives you detail and enables you to write about it, or write about it from a fresh point of view. I think poetry is a single stream, swollen and nourished by every poet who ever lived. There's a beautiful poem by Carlos Martínez Rivas, "Requiem for the Death of Joaquín Pasos," that says poets are like roosters singing out and answering one another in time, in history.

• *Daisy, do you read poetry to your comrade?*

Daisy: Almost never. We used to, we used to share that more often. But now the revolution demands so much from every one of us, there's so little time . . .

• *And to your daughter?*

Daisy: To my daughter, yes. My daughter already has a concept of the word *poet.* For her it's synonymous with friend, or some-one very important, someone she should take into account. I read her poems about things I think are simple enough for her to understand, or poems I know she doesn't understand but which I give her in order to educate her ear. Educate her to the musicality of poetry. She already knows some verses by heart. Last year I took her to Havana with me, and Ernesto arrived; then Cintio and Fina.[2] When they saw her they said, "Oh, how cute," or something like that, and she asked me, "Who are they?" I told her they were both poets. And Cintio said, "Surely, she can't know what a poet is!" "What do you mean," she said, "I do too know what a poet is. And I even know some poems! I'm going to recite *The Heron* by Coronel Urtecho." And she recited it: "High, white winged heron." Cintio and Fina were surprised that a three-year-old child would know about poetry. I hope she'll be a poet . . . or at least that she'll grow up to be a person who recognizes the dignity of the craft, as Fanor Téllez says.

Speaking of Nicaraguan poets I like, there are some young poets I enjoy. Especially Fanor, who unfortunately lives outside

2. Cintio Vitier and Fina García Marruz, Cuban poets.

of Nicaragua. But he's a poet I like a lot. Also Julio Valle; I think he's an extraordinary poet. Very young, but one of those who will leave the strongest testimony of what we're living through at this point in time. Yes, I read poetry to my daughter at night; when I read her her bedtime stories, I often read her poetry as well.

• *Daisy, what was it like for you when your first book of poems was published here? How did people respond to it? Was that a satisfying experience for you?*

Daisy: It's hard to talk about what one feels when one sees one's poems printed in a book. For the first time, you see in concrete form something you've worked so hard on for so many years. I do have a few indicators of the response to that first book. For example, the first edition sold out. That made me happy, not just because it was my own book, but because it means that people are reading poetry, that it interests them.

I've also had some good experiences connected with that book. Do you remember Miriam, the *compañera* who cleaned the offices in the Ministry [of Culture]? One day, Miriam came to me all smiles and said, "You know, there was this guy reading your book on the bus this morning. I wanted to tell him that I work with you, that I know you." She told me about that as something good that had happened to her! For me it was wonderful to think of my poems riding a bus in the hands of someone I didn't even know!

Another anecdote I remember has to do with a mother who told me her son had just come back from the mountains. "I was unpacking his things," she said, "putting away his uniform and all, and what do you think I found? Your book! All wet, wrinkled, squashed. He had your book with him the whole eight months he was in the mountains!"

A *compañera* from the ministry came one day and told me she had just attended a commemorative ceremony for a combatant friend of hers who was killed on the border. And she said they read some of his letters and things he'd written. In one of his letters, there was a whole poem of mine. The publication of that book seems worthwhile to me, for that if for nothing else.

The fact that comrade in the mountains found something useful in one of my poems. That's the kind of communication that makes publishing worth it. It's wonderful to know you can be useful to people in that way. That's what I feel about the poets who nourish me, and I love having the possibility of doing the same—even if it's to a much lesser extent—for others.

• *Have you ever wanted to write prose, Daisy—or essays, plays, something besides poetry?*

Daisy: Once I set some of my poems to music, but I've never sung them. A friend of mine helped me for a while. She had a very good voice and we taped them. But they were just experiments. Later, I wrote some prose. Very little. Mainly for the kind of events in which I had to participate, when I was in the ministry. I wrote an essay about women's poetry in Nicaragua. And some short things. Nothing important. Lately I've been thinking I'd like to write, or try to write, something in prose. Maybe a short story, just to see if I can. Once I dabbled in painting, ceramics. But it was just a hobby. I admire writers who are versatile. Like Yevtushenko. He's done so many things; the last I heard he was making a film. I've always admired artists like that, who have the ability to express themselves in many different ways. I really don't know at this point whether I could ever do that or not.

I've really been obsessed with poetry. I might even say that almost everything I read is verse. I don't mean to say that essays and prose don't interest me. When I was a little girl I thought I could do anything . . . and I wrote poetry, I called myself a poet, I directed little plays, I sang. But who can say whether the very pressure of the Somoza dictatorship didn't diminish our expressive power over all those years, make us more mature before our time? We were forced to do other things, which turned out to be vitally important.

The News Vendor

"POLIO ERADICATED

134,000 ACRES TURNED OVER TO PEASANTS
15,600 PLOTS AND HOMES FOR THE POOR
52,000 FAMILIES RECEIVE DRINKING WATER
13,000 MORE GET ELECTRICITY
LAND USURPED IN THE PAST TO BE RETURNED TO MISKITOS
    AND SUMOS"

Night already
        under the stoplight
        his face yellow
red, green
        and yellow again:

"THOUSANDS GO TO PICK COFFEE
    A THOUSAND SOMOZA MEN ATTACK FROM HONDURAS
    BLOOD OF SEVENTY-FIVE CHILDREN SHED IN THE MOUNTAINS
    COFFEE HARVEST CONTINUES DESPITE ATTACKS"

With his plastic bag wrapping
the last papers of the day
        and his shirt
like a sail flapping
        over the frailness of his body:

"STOP AGGRESSION FROM HONDURAN TERRITORY
    18 SOLDIERS FALLEN IN THE NORTH
    DISTRIBUTION OF SOAP, OIL, FLOUR NATIONALIZED
    TENANTS TO HAVE OWN HOMES
    JOIN THE COTTON BRIGADES
    COFFEE HARVEST, TRIUMPH OF THE PEOPLE"

A poor angel
proclaimer of history
    eyes brilliant from lack of sleep:

"DRY YOUR TEARS TO IMPROVE YOUR AIM
  JUSTICE WILL BE DONE
         AND IT WILL BE FINAL."

Girl with a Parasol

In yellow overalls
she crosses the street
—her hips swaying with the rhythm
    of her step—
her back wet
    beneath her red blouse
and the great sunflower
    of her parasol.

Francisco de Asís Fernández

To change people's sensibility

"I was born in a wonderful land inside another wonderful land, because my home was like a universe. A universe where my father and mother and about forty other people lived: my aunt Mercedes, my aunt Chana, my aunt Haydita. The house had three patios with four galleries around each one, and so many flowers; beautiful gardens. Poetry, literature, art in all its forms flourished in that house. Because my father was a man who dedicated himself exclusively to poetry. He lived and breathed it. When he died we put an inscription on his tombstone which reads: 'Enrique Fernandez Morales: inhabitant of the five continents of art.' "

It's Francisco de Asís Fernández speaking; "Chichí," as his friends call him. I went to see him at his office, the modest room in a modest building which is the Nicaraguan Committee for Friendship with the Peoples. Chichí has held a variety of positions since the Sandinista victory: he was Secretary of the Ministry of the Interior, director of the penitentiary system, and head of the Institute for the Study of Sandinism. The work he's doing now has much more to do with his main task throughout the last years of struggle: solidarity work, both on the part of the Nicaraguans toward the peoples of the world and channeling the solidarity of the peoples of different countries with the Sandinista cause.

When I asked if he'd given some thought to the interview we were about to do, he said that if he had he wouldn't have gone drinking the night before. Nevertheless, he laughed and indicated he was willing to begin. I wanted him, first, to continue evoking that rich world of images and sensibility, such an integral part of his childhood in Granada.

Chichí: In the middle of the first patio there was a kind of kiosk. That's where the orchestra would play, when they held those huge parties in the old days. There was also a chapel where Mass was held. Many priests would come, and many of them were guests at the house. They came to say Mass for my grandmother, who couldn't get out of her brass four-poster canopied bed toward the end. My memories of childhood include daily gatherings of poets, who would meet at our house to argue or defend a poem. And there were terrible fights. I remember Ernesto Cardenal, Carlos Martínez Rivas, Francisco Pérez Estrada, Pablo Antonio Cuadra, José Coronel Urtecho, Carlos Cuadra Pasos—Pablo Antonio's father—and Rodolfo Sandino (who used to write). And there were painters: Peñalba, Omar de León.

All the writers and painters in this country met at my father's house to drink and visit with their women: Ernesto Cardenal met with Adelita Marenco; Carlitos with Irma Prego. They invented different activities, seminars in the summers; in short, my father's whole life was art, and he transformed everything he touched into poetry and love.

My childhood home was a museum. The relics were innumerable. They included things like the first painting ever made in Nicaragua, at the end of the sixteenth century: a painting on wood of the Virgin, St. Joseph and the Child by an anonymous artist. And hundreds of other paintings, religious art of the seventeenth and eighteenth centuries, as well as paintings which began to be identifiable by the artists' names: Pedro Santelis, Adolfo León, Toribio Jerez, the first great Nicaraguan painters. There were portraits of my grandparents, portraits of my great-grandparents, and portraits of my great-great-grandparents—as well as many which had nothing to do with our

family. My father invented names for them: "Mr. So-and-So," "Doña Chepa Chamorro," "Don Juan Arguello," "Doña Berna-bela de la Cerda." He gave them the namès that occurred to him, and there was no one to contradict him. He had great authority in the house. But he always tried for the best name. He did a lot of research, and when he couldn't find out the real name, he'd invent one, one he thought appropriate to the personality he saw in the portrait. My childhood was very much of the provinces, too, with tales of the haunted wagon, legends, spells, the headless priest.

• *Were you an only child?*

Chichí: No. I have a sister two years older than me. And we had a younger sister who died when she was eight months old, thirty-six years ago, around this time of year. Carlos Martínez

Rivas just wrote a poem for her a couple of months ago. Her name was Blanca Fernández, that sister of mine who died. And her death is one of my earliest memories. My sister and I were drawing in one of the galleries, lying on the bricks making pictures, and suddenly we heard my mother and father crying. We ran into the bedroom and saw them embracing each other, crying and looking over at my dead sister. When they saw us they told us to get out. "You have no business being here," they said. We went back to our drawings, but that scene remains engraved on my memory. It's like a photograph, a little yellowed with age, but indelible.

My childhood was such a rich one. I think that's the richest zone one has—the childhood territory—because it's where one begins to form one's sensibility, fascinated by the world, by everything in the world, and learning about everything. And the world they taught me was one of chapels, oil paintings, García Lorca, Cervantes, Neruda. Poets from other parts of the world, and loved by all Nicaraguans, came to my home; men like León Felipe. Flamenco dancers like Carmen Amaya. As a result, I often feel like a great circus tent today, with many people circulating within me, and filled with love for all those who are inside: my memories, the people I care about.

• *I was going to ask you when you began to write, Chichí. Within that world of poetry and art. But when you told me you were drawing pictures when your little sister died, you gave me an image of someone who has exercised his creativity from the time he was very young. Can you remember exactly when it was that you first began taking seriously the craft of poetry, as something specifically yours?*

Chichí: I guess my older sister and I just grew up with poetry. We always felt it as a presence. As a matter of fact, it was she who showed promise as a poet; I was the one who liked to draw. I must have been sixteen or seventeen when I began to take writing seriously. My parents separated and I had to go to Mexico with my mother. That was a very painful time for me. They didn't know how to deal with the situation, and mostly they competed for us. They were always putting us between the devil and the deep blue sea, as the saying goes. For example, my father would kidnap us and take us to some farm he still had in those days. Then my mother would find out where we were, and she'd come loaded down with gifts to win us over. I remember once they even asked us: Well, who do you want to go with, who do you love more? That's still a painful memory. Since I was younger than my sister, I just said: With whomever Marineida wants. Marineida chose my mother, and my father broke down right there and cried.

So that's how we went to live with my mother in Mexico, and we spent some time in the United States too. But I came back to Nicaragua for a vacation once, and showed my father a few of my first poems. That's when he told me I shouldn't go back. He felt I should go on writing, and that if I went back to my mother it would mean the end of poetry for me. Because he said my mother had never understood poetry. That seemed to be one of their problems. I came back then and started studying theater here, and writing poetry. My first poems were published in *La Prensa Literaria:* "Jolen's Biography" and "My Cousin Chale."

Then, in 1964, I went to Madrid. My father arranged for me to study theater there. I audited some courses in literature and art history. And I visited all our poet friends who were in Spain at the time: Luís Rosales, Fernando Quiñones, Félix Grande. We lived a totally bohemian life. You might say that in those days all I lived for was to drink and make love. I had no greater concern than that.

I think I married the first time to escape from that drunken world. It was the drunkenness of poetry, not the drunkenness of the drunk. But it was as if a devil was inside me. And I had to get rid of it to achieve a kind of stability. So I looked for stability in marriage. I married a Puerto Rican woman and we had a son, who is now a beautiful young man sixteen years old. He's named Francisco de Asís Fernández, like me, and he lives with his mother in Puerto Rico.

In 1968 we went briefly to Mexico, and then to Puerto Rico. There I opened a cafe-theater, with Topo Cabán (the Carlos Mejía Godoy of Puerto Rico) and Edwin Reyes, a poet who's a member of the Puerto Rican Socialist Party. We opened the cafe and lived like one big family: it was a meeting place for all the *independentistas* on the island: the painters, the poets, Lorenzo Maro, Rafael Rivera Rosa, the poets from Guajana, Pedro Juan Soto . . . and that's when my life began to change radically.

When one is an artist, when one has an artist's sensibility, perhaps that makes human relationships deeper as well, and then one can understand human problems and social problems better. But in Puerto Rico, I realized all that's not enough. One had to try to understand the political and economic forces that move the world. In Puerto Rico I woke up to the fact that it's not love alone that makes the world go round. And I began reading Nicaraguan history: *The Crazy Little Army* and *The General of Free Men* by Gregorio Selser. Ironically, outside my country I woke up to the deepest feelings about my country. And from that moment on, I had no taste at all for Puerto Rico.

I began to confront my own conscience. I remember I lived in the house where Pedro Albizu Campos had lived; it was a real gesture on the part of the Puerto Ricans, letting me live in that house, the place where the 1950 shoot-out had taken place. And it was in that house on the corner of Sol and Cruz streets that I really committed myself to the Puerto Rican independence movement and the Nicaraguan Revolution. We packed our bags and came home.

I remember being really affected by the fact that many of my Puerto Rican friends knew more about Nicaragua than I did. I was impressed when I heard Angel Rama[1] talking about Solentiname, about Ernesto Cardenal's experience there. And I was taken aback that I didn't even have any idea how strong the Sandinista National Liberation Front was. It wasn't part of my reality then that here in my own country people were fighting and were dying, that we had a Somoza who could not remain in power, and that every one of us had to contribute what we could to the struggle to free Nicaragua. So, in 1970, we packed our bags and returned.

We wanted to do revolutionary theater here, and we wanted to hook up with the FSLN. And about that time I met one of the

1. Angel Rama, Uruguayan writer and critic, recently dead in a plane crash in Madrid.

people who has meant the most to me in my life, Camilo Ortega. It was a real stroke of luck. Through Camilo I came to know the FSLN. At first we were just friends. We hung out together, double-dated, went on excursions to Diriá, to the lagoon there with Carlitos Alemán,[2] and we met at Leonel Vanegas's place.[3] In fact, it was at Leonel's that I first met Camilo. And then we decided that one of the things we could do was to revive the Praxis Group.[4] When Alejandro Aróstegui came back to Nicaragua we went looking for him and said we wanted to revive Praxis, but this time as a project of the FSLN.

• *When did the Praxis Group get off the ground?*

Chichí: In the early sixties was its first period. But it deteriorated. It even went so far as to begin working with the Ministry of Education. And under Somoza that kind of thing made any group suspect, for people with any sense of dignity. So it was a matter of reviving Praxis but of recovering its prestige. As an FSLN project. It was an important cultural experience here. We put out two issues of *Praxis* magazine. Camilo was our contact with the Front.

Then Camilo went underground, and we were left without our contact—as well as without his friendship. Camilo had left me hooked up with René Núñez, but he disappeared too. I didn't see him again until 1973.

In 1972 we were taking part in the campaign to free the political prisoners. And we were writing poetry that called into question the poetic stance of the old Nicaraguans. At that time I wrote a series of poems called *The Constant Blood.* And my first book, *Principio de Cuentas [Initial Scoreboard],* was published in Mexico by Finistierre. Ernesto Mejía Sánchez thought of the title, and the book was illustrated by José Luís Cuevas.[5]

2. Carlos Alemán Ocampos, Nicaraguan ethnologist and writer.
3. Leonel Vanegas, Nicaraguan painter.
4. Alejandro Aróstegui, Nicaraguan painter who was one of the founders of Praxis. Praxis was a group of painters and poets that enjoyed a first period of activity and was later revived as one of the really important groups of creative people working to free Nicaragua from the Somoza dictatorship.
5. José Luís Cuevas, one of Mexico's best artists.

I also worked in advertising during that whole period, in order to support myself. I did advertising for the BANIC Group.[6] Then the earthquake happened, and we went to work with the victims in Grenada. Another poet, Gioconda Belli, was working with the earthquake victims there, too. And one day Bayardo Arce[7] told me: "I have instructions from Ricardo Morales Avilés that you are to go to the university, to work full-time with the Front, but in the university context." So I got a job as a professor of publicity. But I was really working for the FSLN.

By that time I had met my present *compañera*, Gloria Gabuardi.[8] Gloria and I were a much more suitable couple than I had been able to make with my first wife. She had a great respect for literature and art, and she was a revolutionary. Like myself, when we met she was a member of the Sandinista National Liberation Front. There were no contradictions in our political life. It was a happy day when we met. We now have two children: Enrique Faustino (named Enrique after my father and Faustino after my maternal grandfather) and Camilo René (named after Camilio Ortega and René Núñez and René Vivas[9], all three of whom have meant a great deal to me in my life). There was a time when Gloria was underground when she even used the name René herself, as a pseudonym, in honor of the two Renés.

I continued working at the university. Those were the days of the great campaigns to free Chico Ramírez and Efraín Nortalwalton. And I was writing poems which, at that time, Ricardo Morales called ethical poems. It was only much much later that I really understood his criticism. They were poems that attempted to be "political poems," in the most clichéd ways. They lacked freshness because they were made "for" the people and not "from" the people. Now I realize Ricardo was always trying to tell me to write *from* the people and not "for" the people.

6. BANIC, Bank of Nicaragua; then a private firm, now part of the nationalized banking system.

7. Bayardo Arce, today a member of the FSLN's National Directorate.

8. Gloria Gabuardi, Nicaraguan poet.

9. René Vivas survived the struggle and today is a commander and the head of the Sandinista Navy.

Ricardo was one of the lights of Sandinista thought. He was a comrade who always gave you the feeling he'd been looking for you, so you could tell him your troubles. When he showed up one day at my house in Granada, he told me: "When the revolution comes to power, this house will have to become a museum. Don't think you're going to be able to keep on living here," he'd tell me, half joking and half serious. Ricardo was an intellectual who used words with tremendous precision.

When they killed Ricardo, Bayardo told me: We have to publish all his work. I took his manuscripts to Pablo Antonio Cuadra, and he said he wasn't going to publish a word. They're not any good, he said. I remember I left his office in tears of rage that day. Ernesto Cardenal was at Pablo's office when I came in, and I remember he said: "Well, what did you expect? This is *La Prensa*, you know."

It wasn't until years later that we were finally able to publish Ricardo's work. After the victory. When I was director of the Institute for the Study of Sandinism, we began doing his collected works. When Ricardo died, I wrote a poem for him called "Cold Blood." I remember I read it before a great many comrades, in a patio in front of the CUUN offices, at the university. I almost broke down and cried again.

When they killed Ricardo it was a real blow for the Front. At the funeral, I could hardly see for the tears. My comrades said, "Stop crying. You're giving yourself away." "Let them kill me too, then," I answered. I was really shaken. I don't think I've ever felt the kind of pain I felt when Ricardo died.

Later on, we went to Mexico. That was mid-1974. Gloria and I went together and began setting up the solidarity structures there for the FSLN. We met many writers and used our literary relationships as a cloak for our work. We invited Carlos Pellicer[10] to be president of the Solidarity Committee, and we contacted Thelma Nava.[11] Thelma and Adalberto Santana were

10. Carlos Pellicer, one of Mexico's most important twentieth-century poets, was a staunch supporter of the Sandinistas until his death in 1979.

11. Thelma Nava, Mexican poet, coordinated the Mexican Committee of Solidarity with the Nicaraguan People.

the first two who were recruited by the Front for solidarity work
in Mexico; they still work hard for us today.

• *Did you already have your children?*

Chichí: Not yet. We were trying. Gloria became pregnant
during one of the most difficult periods. We lived in a tiny
maid's room on a fifth or sixth floor walk-up. There was no
toilet or bathtub. She had to go up those stairs every day with
her enormous belly. And we slept on a sofa. It got to the point
where I had to sleep on the floor because we couldn't all fit on
the sofa—her belly, her, and me.

I remember one very funny thing about that time. Enrique
Lacayo Farfán, one of the old leaders of the opposition to
Somoza, was a doctor. He was exiled in Mexico, and we began
going to him so he could see Gloria during her pregnancy. But
Enrique was pretty old by that time. He never was able to practice in Mexico because they never gave him permission. We'd
go to see him for Gloria's prenatal appointments, and then we'd
start talking politics. We'd talk about the Front, Somoza, the
National Guard. And after about an hour Enrique would suddenly ask: "And why was it you came to see me, my girl? Do
you have malaria?" He'd forgotten why we'd come. We
couldn't really count on Lacayo Farfán for a systematic checkup
for the coming of Enrique Faustino. We had to change doctors.
But we kept on going to see him and telling him he was really
her doctor, so as not to hurt his feelings. Unfortunately, he died
without seeing the triumph of the revolution.

And so we lived in Mexico for many years. And gradually we
managed to build up a solidarity network, in line with the level
of struggle back home. I can remember when we had to go out
begging just to be able to have Carlos Mejía Godoy sing somewhere; nobody knew who he was. But a few years later we had
relations with the PRI[12] and could get tens of thousands of
people out into the streets in support of Nicaragua, involving all
the political parties and all the labor unions.

12. PRI, Institutional Revolutionary Party, the party in power in Mexico
since the end of the 1910 revolution.

Exile is a painful experience, but I believe it was less painful for those of us who left Nicaragua during that period, because we were able to have a permanent relationship with what was happening inside the country. I think it must have been much harder for people like Concha Palacios—a doctor, who was like a mother to us—or Edelberto Torres, who is a father to all us Sandinistas. Or for Lacayo Farfán. When they left Nicaragua, an organization like the FSLN didn't yet exist.

In Mexico we also founded the committee for Latin American Solidarity, in October of 1977. There was Pablo González Casanova from Mexico, Genaro Carnero Checa from Peru, Francisco Juliaou from Brazil, Carlos Quijano from Uruguay, Rodolfo Puigrós from Argentina, Gabriel García Márquez from Colombia, Jorge Turner from Panama. Toward the end of the war I went to Costa Rica. There, I headed a camp where the comrades going to the southern front spent some time, getting a certain amount of training that we were able to give them. There were some five or six hundred comrades at a time. We gave them a brief introduction to class struggle, Nicaraguan history, the history of the FSLN and its strategy. Sometimes we were able to give a course that lasted fifteen days, but most of the time—and toward the end—it was more like four or five.

Later, when René Núñez entered the country, he left José Pasos and me in charge of the work in Costa Rica. At the very end I worked on a newspaper—Sergio de Castro was the director—which was really the revolution's first open paper. It was called *Patria Libre.* When we finally came across the border, we just handed that paper out to everyone, everyone we saw in the streets.

- *When did you arrive in Nicaragua?*

Chichí: It must have been the 22nd or 23rd of July. It was the most incredible experience I've ever had. We came in a plane, with a great many other *compañeros.* When we landed here at the airport, the first thing we saw was a huge banner that read: WELCOME TO FREE NICARAGUA! FREE HOMELAND OR DEATH! And everyone was shouting slogans. We were coming home, to our own country! The first thoughts I had were of Ricardo,

Julián Roque, Armando Talavera, Camilo—our brothers, all our brothers and sisters who didn't live to see the victory. And everyone who had struggled, as far back as we can remember, so someday we could have this freedom, and didn't live to see it.

And I felt like they were all right here. In the faces of all the comrades and combatants, I saw the faces of those other brothers and sisters who hadn't lived to see this. I felt like my heart was tied into a tight, tight knot. I rode from the airport to Managua in a minibus that Roberto Calderón provided. My heart ached and I felt like I couldn't speak. That's the way it was. It was as if all of a sudden the great joy you're feeling pulls away. You're holding it but you can't release it. You can't release it.

The next day I borrowed a car from my brother-in-law, from Gloria's brother, and I went to see my father in Granada. And that was another great emotion, seeing him again. He had been very ill; the war had really gotten to him, and he was under psychiatric treatment. The Guard had run him out of his house; he had had to sell his entire collection of colonial art, all his furniture; and with the moving and all, they stole all his pre-Columbian treasures, many of his paintings, his unpublished poetry, all sorts of things. I found him in a little house, much heavier, and of course when I saw him I almost died of shock and joy. I don't know how long we just stood there, holding one another, almost rocking, he clutching me, both of us crying. And then I couldn't stay. I had to go right back to Managua to begin work. Enormous tasks lay before us.

• *Chichí, since July 1979 you've had a series of different responsibilities: the prison system, the Institute for the Study of Sandinism, and now this solidarity work. I'd like you to try to reflect on what these different tasks have meant for you as a writer, the conflict or lack of conflict they've represented in terms of your poetry. Have you been able to write? Are you writing now?*

Chichí: I'm going through a lot of changes in the way I think about my poetry. From 1970 to the time of our victory, I wrote almost exclusively what you'd call political poetry. And now, with all the polemics going on, all the arguments, the debates about literary work and revolutionary duty, about so-called committed literature, well, I realize that I'm writing poetry that has nothing to do with politics. Oh, once in a while there's an allusion to something political, like in the poem "Memory of the Dream," in which I'm contemplating my sleeping children and suddenly think of Ricardo Morales and some of the other comrades. But it's all got another dimension now.

I think we have to take a new look at art and literature in the revolution. I think it's only natural that many of our writers feel they need to bear historical witness concerning our heroes and martyrs in their literature and art. I think it's wonderful that many writers reflect the revolution's accomplishments in their work. But I also believe that the universe of literature and art must contain something else. It cannot be limited to that. Within the life of the revolution one's own life exists, one's loves, one's problems. That is the world in which we live.

If the writer is revolutionary he or she will write a good poem about whatever topic. And the revolution is not exclusive. To think we can write only about certain themes and problems would be dangerous. We could fall into the trap of "Sandinista

realism"! In Nicaragua today, we must read a lot: fiction, novels, plays, stories. Even if they have nothing to do with revolutionary themes. It's just as bad to read only Lenin as it is never to read Lenin. And Lenin was a great reader of Dostoyevsky, Cervantes, Gogol, Pushkin.

For me, the function of literature and art is to change people's sensibility. That, precisely, is our socially useful function. We cannot put human imagination in a tiny bag. Right now, for example, I'm writing about my childhood, with all the tenderness my memories evoke. At the same time, my most recent poem is called "Tombstones." Here it is. I'll read it to you.

Tombstones

Who remembers those names in life so often spoken?
How were their faces, their hair and features? What
    the timbre of their voices?
One or two generations suffice to blot out signs,
    laughter, grudges.
Only on the most recent graves are flowers,
and cows grazing off grass growing like absence.
Which of these names are suicides?
Which immaculate virgins, dead in the anguish
of a lonely bed, disheveled with dreams and sleeplessness?
What did they hoard, so greedily, in hovels or palaces?
Surely those loved most who saw through good.

August 19, 1983

Milagros Palma

All that which belongs to us

"I realized that if I wanted to study I had to begin by studying my own language. I barely knew how to write. I had to begin all over again. It was terrible for me, it was hard, but little by little I began with Spanish grammar and discovered as I went along that it's a beautiful thing to study one's own language. That I was already beginning to understand a great deal."

Milagros Palma has taken the American eagle as her own. She has understood what it signals in affliction for the peoples of her continent, and she has gone beneath that. With Rubén Darío, she says: "Eagle, the Condor exists; he is your brother in the heights."

This Nicaraguan from León answered my call with some hesitation. She said she didn't really consider herself a writer: "Maybe it wouldn't be a very interesting interview." But I insisted, and a few days later went to see her at her home in Altamira, where she does her research "always close to the kitchen," and a few steps away from her husband and collaborator Claude Feuillet, who paints a world of images that complement her texts. Their two children complete the passionate space of this house.

We taped the conversation on a cool terrace behind the main part of the dwelling.

Milagros: Well, I'm from León. The León of the *Gigantona,* of the *Toro Guaco,* the festivals of *San Jerónimo,* the festivals of *Guadalupe,* the *Inditas,* the *Purísmas.* I come from the León of Rigoberto López Pérez, of the terror of July 23rd, the massacre of the students.[1] That was the León in which I lived, and which I took with me when I graduated from school. I was graduated from the institute high school there, but before that I had worked at the Union House, teaching in order to help support my studies. And to help my family, too. Because we were a large family. There were fourteen of us.

• *How old were you when you left León?*

Milagros: I was eighteen. It was 1968. But I didn't just leave León. I left Nicaragua. I went to Chicago, and those were the years of the extreme racial conflicts and all. I worked in a factory there, but I didn't last more than a year. With what I was able to save, I went to Europe. I had a brother in Paris who had followed more or less my same itinerary; he had gone off, like I did, to work. So I went to France and my brother, who was a teacher at the Sorbonne by that time, helped put me through school.

• *Don't tell me you began studying anthropology just like that! From a factory in Chicago to the Sorbonne?*

Milagros: No. It wasn't that simple. I began studying biochemistry because that was popular when I was in the institute. I thought it would be a good thing, useful, to study biochemistry. But I couldn't make heads or tails of it. Because, and this was something I came to understand much later, I hardly knew how to read. I had almost never opened a book, except for my textbooks. That was a tragedy for me because I didn't know

1. The *Gigantona* is a folk figure, a large doll that people take into the streets during festivities, especially in León. The *Toro Guaco* is another such figure. *San Jerónimo, Guadalupe,* and *Las Inditas* are religious festivals. The *Purísmas* are the Marianist devotion in early December to the Virgin Mary. Rigoberto López Pérez was the patriot who in 1956 shot the first Somoza. The shooting took place in León. And on July 23, 1959, a student demonstration was massacred by the National Guard in León.

how to study. I didn't have the skills; I had never developed them. So finally I realized that in order to study what I wanted I had to begin by studying my own language. I had to begin all over again. It was hard, but little by little I began with the Spanish and as I went along I discovered that it's a beautiful thing to study one's own language; I was beginning to understand so many things. And I ended up with a master's degree in Spanish, there in France.

• *Interesting that you had to go to France in order to learn Spanish!*

Milagros: Yes, and what surprised me most was that the French spoke a better Spanish than I did. How is it possible, I would say to myself, that I've never been taught all this? Spanish is a beautiful language! When you know how to speak it well, you can really express yourself! It was like being liberated. So I came back to Nicaragua, but with a whole new set of plans. I had studied Spanish, but then I began to get into linguistics in more depth, to learn where language itself came from. I began with the historical problem of language: how the concepts are formed, thought itself; in short, what we call "culture." Because a language reflects an entire vision of the world. I discovered that language is history. I discovered ethnolinguistics. I returned to Nicaragua in 1975, with Claude and our first son.

• *Did you start right in at the university here?*

Milagros: I started working at the National University, first teaching Spanish in the basic program; and that's where I was faced with what had been my own problem: students who hardly knew how to read. That was a big topic of discussion at that time. Nineteen seventy-six was a very effervescent year here. A lot of struggle. At the same time, I had a research project going, about oral tradition. I wanted to discover more about that identity that I had found and spent so much time examining overseas; it was something I felt necessary in the consolidation of my own identity. And it also allowed me to give something which might be positive, might shed some light on all that which belongs to us but about which there has been so much prejudice. All that which people lump together and call "folklore." And I came up with an entirely new vision.

So, on the one hand, I was teaching, and on the other, doing research. I went on like that, traveling around the country with my husband Claude. He got excited about all the popular man-ifestations of culture that there are in Nicaragua, and he painted while I was doing my research. But the situation finally got to the point where we had to leave again, because there was a strike at the university. I got desperate. I felt I would die if I stayed. It was terrible.

• *Milagros, did you participate in the struggle, in the the political struggle, in any way, during those years?*

Milagros: I participated some, but never in an organized way. My attitude, my research, my conversations with the peasants—searching for their history—made me feel that I was an accomplice of all this that was taking place. But the truth is I was just doing the work I'd set out to do. Sometimes I would go to Ometepe, to the small villages there, and it became a conflictive situation because people believed I was underground or that I was involved in political work and didn't want to say. I wasn't really involved in political work as such; I was just doing my research. But here in Nicaragua they could as easily kill you because they suspected you of something as if you were really involved.

So we went to Colombia. And we continued the same kind of work down there. We were working in the Amazon region with the indigenous peoples. We were involved in a project on the problem of the extermination of the native peoples, the history of four hundred years of continuous extermination. And it seemed important to begin to work on what all those religious sects appearing as missionaries, as linguists, were really doing; the Summer Institute of Linguistics, above all: appearing to make a scientific contribution while what they were really doing was counterrevolutionary spying, on the one hand, and on the other, subjecting the native peoples to the most profound misery, forcing them to live on charity, making them pray, that is, providing them with a practice that aided them—the so-called missionaries—in their own political objectives.

There, I made a series of learning cards. Because what the "missionaries" did more than anything was translate the Bible into the indigenous languages. So I tried to make for them teaching materials based on their own traditions, their own myths, so they would have their own texts to read, their own culture. I wasn't working alone; I was training a group of students from the University of the Andes. Until it seemed I had nothing more to do there—by then, there were enough Colombians who had a new perspective on anthropological work—and so I left. What we had done, more than anything, was turn history upside down, do away with all those prejudices which have plagued the native from the very moment of the Spanish conquest. What we did was give the people a new set of values, through becoming acquainted with their own thought, their own philosophy of life. And all this was consolidated to a certain extent in a first book, *Mythical Words of the People of Water*. The anthropological text was combined with paintings, to make it more graphic.

I knew that language had been studied with the vision of the colonizer, the way it's been done with Quechua, with Nahuatl; or as it's done in the Summer Institute of Linguistics. Once I had students working in that part of the Amazon, I could go on to other areas. And I began to think it would be important to work with the condor. Because with all the multinational corporations, a series of symbols have been introduced; the eagle is a symbol of imperialism, and it appears even in advertising to the extent that it confuses us in our own symbolic values, and it distorts the symbols we've inherited from pre-Columbian times.

I wanted to retrieve the image of the condor, for the sake of the cohesion and consolidation of our Latin American identity. But I wanted to retrieve it through collecting stories, speaking to peasants, mestizos and native peoples—because they are the ones who remember the condor in its past dimension. I collected several myths, which allowed me to develop an approach—to interpret them a little in the light of this whole identity problem of ours, to expose them and give them back to the Colombian people. And I wanted to gain time against what was being done with the eagle. Because I felt it was terrible that those symbols were being erased, as it were. There's a clear-cut policy of destroying all those elements which might permit the consolidation of our authentic identity.

Popular cultural manifestations have been studied from the point of view of the European, of the foreigner, but now we Latin American anthropologists must study them in the context of our own problems, with an eye toward recovering them and promoting the consolidation of our whole process of developing a national identity, a Latin American identity. Because in each of the Latin American countries there are peasants, native peoples, with a common symbolic language. It is the language of an oppressed people. That's what we must rescue. I believe it's something fundamental within our revolutionary process.

• *Milagros, how and when did you return to Nicaragua the second time?*

Milagros: Well, I was only waiting to complete that book about the condor, because it was important to Colombia and important to us as Nicaraguans as well. And then we came home. Here I began working at the Central American University. I am teaching, but my main task is still research. I'm going back over all that work I did in 1976 and '77 to see if it's still valid, to try to place it in a revolutionary context and see what value it has for the struggle taking place here now.

• *Are you getting support for this work? Do you feel there's a sufficient degree of understanding of its importance?*

Milagros: There's a certain level of understanding. For example, I think it's important that the work is being published in *Ventana*.[2] It gives me a great deal of satisfaction that the people can read about their own personages, begin to understand their own myths, in a society which has perpetuated and transmitted its values and knowledge only through the oral tradition. We're making a good beginning. But I think there's still a great deal of work that must be done in the area of research. We need a new *attitude* about research here in Nicaragua. Because we have a lot of people who love the *idea* of research; they get excited about a project. But research can't be improvised; it's a discipline.

• *Are you working on a project right now?*

Milagros: I'm waiting for the publication of a new book, a collection of all the pieces that have been published in *Ventana*.

2. *Ventana* is the weekly cultural supplement included in the Saturday issue of *Barricada*, the FSLN's official daily. The original *Ventana*, edited in the sixties at the University of León by Sergio Ramírez and Fernando Gordillo, was the FSLN's first attempt to coordinate a cultural movement in the political context. The new *Ventana* is its successor.

It's called *Along the Pathways of Myth in Nicaragua,* and it includes all the personages. Editorial Nueva Nicaragua is bringing it out.

• *And what kind of response have you had to your work? Do people speak to you about what you're doing?*

Milagros: My greatest satisfaction now is knowing that the very people who have been my informants are reading my work; it's read by ordinary people all over the country, in León, for example, in the working-class neighborhoods. This has to do with the literacy campaign that took place here, the fact that people can read, and they *do* read. It's so impressive. That's been my greatest response.

• *You mean people call you or communicate with you in some way?*

Milagros: Yes. They call me and they have new stories to tell me. Right now I have to make another trip to the island of Ometepe. People have found out I'm back because of the pieces appearing in *Ventana,* and they get in touch with me.

• *Anything else?*

Milagros: I'm also working on another book. I brought the raw material with me from Colombia. But I had put it aside to work with the condor. It's a beautiful work because it's about the indigenous peoples of the Amazon, about a community where the men say they get their wives from the people of the water. What I am trying to do in that book is to show an approach to the thought of that community; to demonstrate the analogy, the logic of their actions within that universe, within that ecosystem which is the jungle, such a hostile environment. That's almost ready to go to the printers as well. It's a book about the travelers of the Great Anaconda. It will be illustrated with Claude's paintings, too.

And I have plans for doing some work on the Miskitos. That's important because the revolution has opened up great prospects for the real participation of all the oppressed cultures within the larger project of our national identity. As an anthropologist, I see that as an urgent necessity. And it should be important for Latin America as a whole.

Julio Valle-Castillo

For me, literature has become a way of understanding the world

Julio Valle-Castillo is a small, slim man—nervous, emphatic and precise in his speech—author of several books, apart from his own poetry, of criticism and literary research. He heads the Ministry of Culture's department of literature, and he is also special advisor to the Minister of Culture, Ernesto Cardenal. In granting this interview, Julio breaks with a self-imposed distance from *Ventana*.[1] He's a storyteller, and I ask him to begin by telling me some stories about his childhood and youth.

Julio: My family comes from that whole accursed middle class, that cushion which absorbs the blows of the class struggle, absorbs them and sometimes muffles them. I was bred a Catholic—though I'm not a practicing believer today—in the classical and classist tradition prevalent here. I was raised by my mother and grandfather, and my grandfather was a very important figure in my life. He was a Liberal,[2] a middle-level peasant who

---

1. Many of these interviews were first published in Spanish in *Ventana*, the cultural supplement of the FSLN's daily *Barricada*. Julio was having a rift with *Ventana* at the time this interview was conducted.

2. Traditionally, as in much of Latin America, the two official political parties were the Liberals and the Conservatives. Somoza was a Liberal. The Conservatives were the bourgeois opposition for the half-century preceding the Sandinista victory.

came to Matagalpa fleeing the persecution unleashed by the Conservatives after the fall of Zelaya in 1909. And he settled in Masaya along with his whole family, his parents and brothers and sisters.

This elderly Liberal was critically important in my life. He gave me a whole set of values which are fundamental to me now. Naturally, being a Liberal, he sided with Somoza, mainly because he had suffered all that persecution on the part of the Conservatives against the Liberals following the intervention of 1912 in Masaya.

And that's what he cultivated in his grandchildren. And in me, especially. A passionate devotion for General Benjamín Zeledón. To him, it was a way of transmitting his anti-imperialism. I don't think he ever really came to understand what Sandino was all about. On the other hand, I have an uncle who was baptized César Augusto, after Sandino. But now they just call him Carlos. Anyway, my grandfather had a series of moral values that are important to me, and I think they're something I've wanted to hang onto. Because I believe that revolutionary commitment begins with a sense of decency. Not only from a political understanding, but from simple decency. And that was something my grandfather gave me. Since my father left home when I was very young, my grandfather was the man in our house.

• *That seems so common here in Nicaragua, the father abandoning the family . . .*

Julio: It is common. My father is a good man, his name is Julio Valle, just like me. We're friends now, but I get along much better with my mother. My mother is a homebody, a seamstress; sometimes she paints primitive paintings, and she's a woman who's come to understand the revolution as the fulfillment of Christian doctrine. My mother is overjoyed when she hears about the giving out of land titles, things like that.

My grandfather, on the other hand, gave me his devotion for Nicaragua's modernist poets, for liberalism, for Zeledón. He was confused; he confused the values of early liberalism with the sellout liberalism of Moncada. But, still, he was a decent man, and were he alive today, I'm sure he'd be with the revolution because of his Christianity.

• *Julio, are you an only child?*

Julio: I'm the only son. I have a younger sister. My sister has been a much freer and more lively spirit than I. I've always been a bit uncomfortable with society, apathetic; my childhood wasn't the typical happy childhood of kids playing in the streets. I never learned how to play baseball. I was a terrible athlete.

• *Where did you study?*

Julio: At the Salesian School. My mother says they sent me there to give me a Christian education. But what they really did was deform me. And because I've been faithful to true Christianity I've broken with the kind they imposed upon me at the Salesian School.

• *So what brought you to poetry, and to the revolution? What changed you?*

Julio: Well, I don't know if what I'm going to say has any scientific validity, but for me it has the validity of experience. Literature has been like a safety valve for me, a safety valve for my soul. And I place the word "soul" in quotes; it's been my way of understanding the world, my way of communicating with people, my way of coming to grips with everything. It's also been my way of breaking with the world, and my way of trying to change it. That's why it was so important for me to have met Ernesto Cardenal.

The first of Ernesto's books I read was called *A Prayer for Marilyn Monroe and Other Poems.* And then I met him at a park here in Managua, where they used to hold exhibits. He was wearing his sandals, his bluejeans and his *cotona* [the cotton smock that's become his trademark], and he had a beard. It was in the month of March, I can't remember whether it was 1966 or 1967. I saw him standing there and I literally began to jump up and down. I must have been about fourteen then. I went up to him and told him how important he was to me.

In Cardenal I found a priest, a poet, and an opponent of Somoza. As a young student at a Catholic school, where they certainly didn't encourage you to oppose Somoza—one still felt it was dangerous, a sin—meeting Cardenal was like a kind of salvation for me. And he's been a decisive influence in my life ever since. To me he's the synthesis of Christian conduct and the honesty that must lead to revolution.

• *Julio, at the age of fourteen, when you first met Ernesto Cardenal, were you already writing poetry?*

Julio: Yes. I was writing in the style of García Lorca. I'd read a lot of Lorca, from the time I was a child, and a lot of Darío as well. I learned Darío from my grandfather. My grandfather didn't sing me to sleep, he recited poems to me when he put me to bed; poems which he considered moral lessons—Darío, Lorca, the Machados, and then all the other great modernist poets.

• *But how did you make the transition from listening to the poetry your grandfather recited to you to something you yourself wanted to produce? How did you begin to write?*

Julio: To my grandfather, the most important people he knew were poets. I don't know if he really believed in them, but he was very proud of his friends who wrote poetry. My grandparents had a big store—they sold clothing, fabric, shoes—there in the Masaya market. I remember a pharmacist who was also a poet; he'd come by. And there was an eccentric poet named Selmo Sequeira who was around then, too. He had been one of the lesser modernists. And another named J. Augusto Flores Z. For my grandfather, the archetypal human being was someone between a priest and a poet.

• *Did you ever think of becoming a priest?*

Julio: Yes, I wanted to be a priest. What happened was I became disillusioned by the Salesians at the school they sent me to. So then I wanted to be a poet, a writer. And it seemed to please my grandfather when I wrote poems. It was my way of identifying with him, and his way of fulfilling himself in me. My grandfather was the only person I can remember who was not against my deciding to become a writer. In fact, he celebrated it.

• *And your first publications?*

Julio: In August of 1968, Camilo Ortega Saavedra was studying at the Salesian School. He was a tall, lanky fellow with a mustache. And we started publishing a magazine together: *Forward* [he takes out a copy from a nearby bookshelf, and begins to leaf through it]. The editor was Camilo Ortega; the assistant editor was Jorge Campbell; and there were others: Olinto Valle, who's in the local government of Masaya today. This is where I published my first poems.

• *So before you went to Mexico, where you lived for so long, you'd already had a literary life in Nicaragua?*

Julio: Yes, I began to have a literary life here in Masaya. In fact, I published my first book here, but it's not a book of poetry.

• *What's it called?*

Julio: *Unmasked Minutes.* It's a study of a modernist poet who used to frequent my house, a friend of my grandfather's, Rafael Montiel. His first book had that title: *Unmasked Minutes.* I knew Montiel; he was the oldest of the poets still writing when I was a child, and he had traveled widely. He wrote a book of narratives called *From Masaya to Masaya by Way of New York.* He also appears in the *Nicaraguan Parnassus,* published in Barcelona by Mauchi Press, in 1912. So I collected his poetry; I felt that critics of Nicaraguan poetry had never had sufficient objectivity with poets like him. I never really went for the criteria of the vanguardists like Coronel Urtecho or Pablo Antonio Cuadra. I didn't like what they had to say about Nicaraguan literature. It would be an exaggeration to say that I understood their opinions politically; I didn't. But I mistrusted them literarily. And that led me to study poets like Montiel.

So I began publishing the work of others, not my own work; and that's been a constant in my production, I think. Other people's work has always been more important to me than my own. I've enjoyed working collectively more than on my own. I guess that's why most of my books have been anthologies, chronologies, works done with other *compañeros.* Among those I've had the privilege of working with are Ernesto Mejía Sánchez, Angel Rama, Lizandro Chávez Alfaro, Jorge Eduardo Arrellano . . .

• *Julio, what was it that took you to Mexico?*

Julio: I had a hard time graduating from high school because I was never any good at math. And I was always an outsider: in my generation, in my family, in my city. The only thing I ever

wanted to do was read, read, read . . . and write. I fought with
the Salesians, too, and I went off to finish my diploma at the
institute in Masaya. I had to learn seventy math problems by
heart, memorize them, but I finally made it. And after all that, I
decided to go to Mexico to study.

• *What year was that?*

Julio: That was 1970. I went to Mexico to study Spanish language and literature at the university, but my real university
turned out to be Mejía Sánchez. I was lucky enough to be close
to him during that period in which he set out to increase his
knowledge of Nicaraguan history. And since he was my professor, I learned along with him.

• *How many years did you remain in Mexico?*

Julio: I stayed until 1979. I got my degree and wrote my thesis,
a complete research project. I also got a scholarship from the
Latin American Writers Community of the Fine Arts Institute;
and I took part in a poetry workshop with Hernán Lavín Cerna,
in the chapel of the old library that had once belonged to Alfonso Reyes. I gave lectures in the provinces as well as in Mexico
City. And I didn't really want to come back to Nicaragua.

In June of 1974 the first Nicaraguan exiles came to mount a
solidarity campaign in Mexico. They were preparing support for
a big action that the FSLN was about to carry out. Of course I
didn't know when or where. Looking back, I'm clear about it all
today. But I was confused at the time. Maybe those first *compañeros* who came to Mexico weren't very skilled in handling
the whole thing. Or maybe I'm not objective enough in judging
them. They were persecuted when they left Nicaragua; they
came from a country where the dictatorship was already escalating the repression; Ricardo Morales Avilés and Oscar Turcios
had already been killed at Nandaime. So those *compañeros*
arrived, and of course they were suffering from all the psychosis
and the pressure of the situation they'd left behind. And they
found me, a kid who delighted in philology, in books, putting
on airs about an erudition I haven't achieved even now. Maybe
they felt I lacked a real passion for the problems of Nicaragua. I

had the clarity but not the passion. And for Nicaraguans, passion is essential.

Sometimes I played the role of cynic with those *compañeros.* And at the same time the role of the skeptic. And so they simply ignored me. Dispensed with me, just like that. But, luckily, those weren't the only *compañeros* in Mexico. And even those comrades who so readily dismissed me, whether they know it or not, did contribute to my understanding of what was going on in my country.

Because, I'll tell you something. I'm a writer; I wanted to be a writer and that's what I am. But without the revolution, more specifically without Sandinism—although I'm not a member of the FSLN—my life would have been meaningless. Sandinism is what's given me coherence, identity, nationality, ethics, and a historical *raison d'être.* Those *compañeros* who came to Mexico in the middle of 1974—whom at first I couldn't understand, nor they me; those *compañeros* who launched the first week of solidarity in Mexico, when Carlos Mejía Godoy came—he wasn't famous then like he is now; those *compañeros* let me read my first poems in favor of the revolution at one of the events that week. From that time on, what I've most wanted has been to reeducate myself in the meaning of Sandinism. And all within the framework of being a writer.

So I came back to Nicaragua in 1979, just in time for the funeral for Commander Carlos Fonseca. In the midst of the rubble, the terrible scars left by the earthquake and the war, walking through the center of the city from Government House to the temporary mausoleum, I saw the new men and women, the members of the National Directorate of the FSLN, the people. My grandfather had already died; I had his permission to change. It was very important for me to feel myself there, among the rubble of a razed city, and to see passing by that "cadaver so full of world," to quote Vallejo.[3]

3. The great Peruvian poet César Vallejo, in his poem "Masas" (November 1938), wrote of "a cadaver so full of world." It's the cadaver of a fighter, and throughout the poem one goes up to him, begging him to get up; then two come, and then a thousand, and finally one hundred thousand. When "everyone in the world" comes to beg the same thing, the cadaver rises.

On the first anniversary of Fonseca's death, in 1977, I had already written a poem that may give you an idea of my evolution, in this sense, or of my understanding of the Nicaraguan process. It's called "History Is Like Carlos Fonseca's Body," and it talks about all the times they reported Carlos as dead: at Chaparral, at Nandaime, at Zinica . . . but every time they went to bury him, or to steal his boots or his knapsack, they found he was alive. So to get back to your question, it was precisely on the day of Carlos's funeral, when they brought his body down from the mountains where he had been killed and buried three years earlier—it was on that day that I entered Managua. And I've been here ever since.

• *And when did you begin work at the Ministry of Culture?*

Julio: The next day, November 9th.

• *As head of the Ministry's Literature Department, it seems to me you've been a part of a number of dreams: the poetry workshops, the Tuesday poetry evenings at the theater, the magazine called* Poesía Libre [Free Poetry]. *What can you tell me about all this work?*

Julio: Well, I'm interested in the poetry workshops, not only because for the first time in Nicaragua they provide the possibility for ordinary people, working people, to have access to poetry, but because of what they assume about that reality with regard to craft. We young poets here have a romantic and sometimes idealistic conception of poetry. Some of my contemporaries write poetry as if they were sitting on an analyst's couch; not just out of necessity (since poetry is always a necessity) but simply out of the need to vent their feelings. But a consciousness of the craft, of the process, leaving the poem to be what it will—the author is simply an instrument—to be able to have a verbal command, a control of your entire arsenal of expression, to be an artist, a craftsperson, to be able to elaborate, erase, erase again, tear it up and start over with a knowledge of what you're doing; that seems of utmost importance to me.

What many call "inspiration" means working as a writer 48 hours out of ever 24, in front of a typewriter. Because to be a writer you have to sit down and write, not just toss off a poem now and then. When one says that literary work is physical work, manual work, it immediately changes your conception of the poetic craft, and by the same token it changes your evaluation of the poet as a citizen incorporated into the revolutionary process. I believe that one of the virtues of the poetry workshops is that they have taught the young poets to tear up their poems, to erase, to correct, to criticize, to listen to other opinions . . .

• *And what about your own work, Julio? What are you working on now?*

Julio: I'm working on several books at once. I'm finishing one called *This Dark Pomegranate;* the title's from Neruda: "So that they may know, if there is doubt, that I have died loving you and you me, if I have not fought at your waist, I leave in your honor this dark pomegranate, this song of love." The book has five parts. The first is called "Tribal Round for the Birth of Sandino"; the second, "Chiefs of Staff, or Altarpiece of Sandino's Men." It's a long poem in praise of Sandino's generals: Pedro Altamirano, Francisco Estrada, Coronado Maradiaga, Socrates Sandino, Juan Pablo Umanzor, Pedro Cabrera. It's an allegory of the mountains and of the people; what goes into making the hero. The third part is an extensive poem called "An Account of the Struggle and Massacre in Monimbó," a poem constructed as if it were a codex, in which the codex is plastic art as well as language. And the people are all there, with their testimony. The fourth part of the book consists of epitaphs, poems in the style of Edgar Lee Masters, which speak of the fifty thousand martyrs of the revolution, a part of the history of the Nicaraguan people. And the fifth part is called "Full Charge": my testimony, in poetry, from my own first notion of death—which I had from the brutal murders under Somoza—until the victory. The book is a bit pretentious.

• *Ambitious, to say the least. It sounds like the book of someone who thinks he may never be able to write anything afterward.*

Julio: I think it's a book that will shut me up for some time. But in this revolution just getting on a bus is like a lifetime. It's enough to go to a market. There's so much, so much . . . I feel that's got to be my reeducation. I must say my *mea culpa* in public. I know that I've devoted myself more to being a writer than to being a revolutionary. I have felt more of an obligation toward writing because I always feel that I'm going to lose it if I don't get it down. I feel everything escaping me. There are moments which hold a world of tremulousness, reverberation, emotion, and if I don't grab them they may become opaque. I'll no longer be able to write them down.

And I'm writing another book, at the same time as the one I just mentioned. It's called *Jubilant Matters*. It's an affectionate, joyful poem about the revolution for my friends, about my friends, about incidents and letters, anecdotes, things that happen. I'm also working on a book of literary investigation, *Literature in Nicaragua*. It will be a collection, from the perspective of the Sandinist People's Revolution, of all the essays on literature written by Nicaraguans, some self-reflection on Nicaraguan creation. And I have a book of prose in the works; it's called *The Crazies*. Portraits of village idiots, those popular madmen and women, those personages who circulate throughout the provinces in Nicaragua. People like life-affirming tragedies because they reaffirm life in the midst of their dispersion and human misery. They are victims of the system, victims of ourselves . . .

• *Julio, with so many books all going at once, and with your work at the ministry, how do you organize your time? How do you handle the creative process? How do you divide your workday, or week?*

Julio: I go to the Ministry of Culture in the mornings. I'm always there in the mornings because I have a lot to do, from proofing and editing, laying out and designing *Poesía Libre* and the other publications, to approving a program or seeing someone. Then, in the evening, when I come home I always write. From six to eight. When I feel like writing, when I have time for it and am able to do it, I also write very early in the morning, from five to six or seven in the morning. And I write on Sundays. Of course, my wife feels I don't give her all the time I should. So sometimes we do things together on the weekends, and on the few vacations I've had. I'd like to write more; that's the truth. Many *compañeros* probably think I've been more faithful to literature than to the revolution. I confess that when it comes down to it, I don't really know where one ends and the other begins.

Tomás Borge

I am a persecuted, underground poet

Tomás Borge Martínez is the elder brother, the extraordinary survivor of more than twenty years of struggle. He is the "old man" on the National Directorate of the Sandinista National Liberation Front. He is the only one left of that trio—Carlos Fonseca, Silvio Mayorga, and himself—that almost a quarter of a century ago had the vision that lit a spark of hope in the eyes of an oppressed people. Then began the long, hard, terrible, crazy, self-sacrificing, almost unimaginable and historic task of changing the face of their homeland.

Tomás is Minister of the Interior in the new revolutionary government. He is the head of State Security, the police, the forces of order . . . and the enemies of the Nicaraguan process never tire of portraying him as a tyrant or dictator. Yet Tomás is someone who radiates love: the initiator of poetry workshops among the country's soldiers; a Minister of the Interior who competes with the Minister of Culture to see who can bring the largest number of foreign artists and intellectuals to Nicaragua.

Tomás, keeper of "law and order," is also the major spokesman for the unique generosity of this revolution. Having suffered imprisonment as few have suffered it—long periods of isolation, severe torture—it is known how he "took revenge" on his torturer by pardoning him. It is also a well-known fact that, when the lackey responsible for the torture and death of his first wife Yelba came to trial, Tomás ordered that he "be accused of all his crimes . . . except those carried out on Yelba."

This man, born in Matagalpa in 1930, surprises one daily with the diverse aspects of his life, details which reveal a man who is as sensitive as he is rigorous, as affectionate as he is profound, as much the poet as the fighter. And it is as a poet that I approach him now. It is as a poet–although he barely accepts the definition–that I requested the interview, asking him to speak of his relationship to the world of books and to his own writing.

The interview took place in Bello Horizonte, a working-class neighborhood to which the leader has recently moved. (During the first three years after the Sandinista victory, Tomás Borge lived in a large house in the elegant residential suburb of Las Colinas, south of the city of Managua. Suddenly, he—along with his wife Josefina, his children, and the "children of the people" who complete his extended family—all moved into this poor neighborhood farther into the capital. Nicaraguans were not surprised.)

Here, then, is our conversation, with few corrections, just as it took place.

• *Tomás, let's begin with your first memories of a literary nature: books, authors, any readings that were done in your home when you were a child. I don't know if in your house people read out loud . . . perhaps you might even have some images that aren't strictly literary, that is to say, that don't come necessarily from books, but which have stayed with you as literary experiences.*

Tomás: My first memories are of books my mother used to read me. They were religious books. I remember very clearly *The Little Flowers,* by Saint Francis of Assisi, which I haven't reread but which evokes in me a kind of nostalgia for what at that time I considered beautiful literature. And which probably is beautiful literature. I remember other religious books, almost always having to do with Saint Francis of Assisi, a saint whom my mother worshiped with particular devotion. I believe, although this may seem like a religious or political profanation, that Saint Francis taught me tenderness.

I was fortunate in that my father owned a considerable library, and he encouraged me to read; prior to adolescence, I especially read Greek and Roman mythology. I don't know why my father was so interested in my reading mythology. I also had access to a great deal of literature in that library of his; the lives of great men, important biographies. And I also remember that he encouraged me to read José Martí, Juan Montalvo, and González Prada, among others.

In my childhood, I read a lot of poetry, too, particularly that of Rubén Darío, the inevitable poet for any Nicaraguan. And even, I remember once as a child I sent some of my own poems to a newspaper, a weekly . . . I don't remember its name. Apart from the humor of GRN, and Manolo Cuadra and other Nicaraguan poets of the times, that weekly published things sent in by its readers. I think it was called . . .

• *Would that have been in Managua?*

Tomás: In Managua.

• *And did they publish your poems?*

Tomás: I don't remember, I don't remember. I guess not, because it was the primitive poetry of a child, not yet influenced by modern literary currents, a literature still perhaps too elementary in terms of its formal character. And besides, I'm no Rubén Darío!

But anyway, I lived among books, and in the first part of my life I was an avid reader of Flaubert, of Victor Hugo—apart from the authors I've already mentioned—of the Russian classical authors, and of Cervantes. And when I was an adolescent, I got enthusiastic about the novels of Jack London and John Steinbeck. It was at that same time that I began to read the novels of Karl May.

• *Yes, in another interview you mentioned that German writer. I don't know him, but from your description he sounds sort of like a European Jack London.*

Tomás: Karl May, being German, and never having been to the United States—something I only recently found out—wrote about the American West. His main characters are Old Shatterhand and Winitu. Winitu was an Indian, and old Shatterhand was an explorer or adventurer in the Far West. The novels of Karl May were structured around certain qualities these men had, in contact with the difficult reality of the American West. That is, the permanent confrontation with injustice, crime, the exploitation of the Indians . . . that is, confronting this whole aberration which was colonialism in the American West. Old Shatterhand and Winitu expressed, in my judgment—unfortunately, I haven't reread Karl May's works; I'd like to get my hands on them again, but that hasn't been possible—they expressed the best qualities human beings ought to have.

Old Shatterhand and Winitu had a tremendous respect, almost a fanatical respect, for personal loyalty, for courage, for generosity, for disregarding danger, and for human solidarity.

• *It's interesting, because the usual "heroes" of the American West are figures like the Lone Ranger and Tonto, figures which have within them all the distorted values of a literature created to support a system—the very name Tonto ("stupid," in Spanish) implies the devaluation of the Indian, and so forth—and here we have a German writer, translated into Spanish, who works with totally opposite values.*

Tomás: The sense I have is that those books were the opposite of Tarzan and Superman. Because their heroes were men who were vulnerable to pain, to the fear of death, to solidarity. Winitu even died in one of the novels, which caused me several months of secret inner mourning, something like an awareness of the futility of sorrow, or perhaps more like a premonition. Afterwards, Winitu was Faustino Ruíz, or perhaps Danto Pomares.[1] For many months I suffered because of Winitu's death and Old Shatterhand's sorrow. So that these characters, as I remember them, are antithetical to the characters created by the cheap new American literature in order to glorify the domination of the white race and of Americans in relation to the backward and poor peoples of this earth.

• *Tomás, when I asked for this interview, your first answer was "I'm not a writer," and you repeated that just now, before we got started. Of course, you are a great deal more, and the main tasks you've had to assume are different ones. But for me,* Carlos, the Dawn Is No

1. Faustino Ruíz was one of the earliest members of the FSLN. He died in the Pancasán guerrilla in 1967. Danto (or Germán) Pomares was also one of the important FSLN leaders. He died in battle shortly before the end of the war in 1979.

Longer beyond Our Reach[2] *is one of the great poems to have come out of the Nicaraguan Revolution. Did you at any time in your life want to be a writer, or a poet?*

Tomás: It's true, I'm not a writer. Most of the things that have been published have not been things I have written, but rather things I have said. In any case, I express my own ideas primarily in oral form.

But when I was an adolescent I wanted to be a priest. My mother was very enthusiastic about the idea of me being a priest, but when the eyes of the women around my neighborhood began to shine for me in a special way, I decided, because of personal honesty, not to become a priest. I understood at that moment that I did not have the vocation to carry out the vow of chastity, and I renounced that possibility.

And of course, like every boy, I dreamed of becoming a pilot, and flying through the air in an airplane.

Afterward, the political situation in Nicaragua led me into political struggle and into revolutionary struggle, and the desires I had first about becoming a priest and then about sailing through the air were neutralized by a clear vocation to participate in the struggle of our people against the Somoza dictatorship . . . and then against imperialist domination.

If you ask me now, at this point in time, what I would liked to have become, I've already said it—and you have it there in one of your questions: I would like to have been a film director.

I think film is the highest form of art; a complete art, as some say. In any case, it's an art form as exciting as the eyes of a woman looking into your own; it's the possibility of developing all of a human being's creative capacity, of putting the imagination, and the reality we sometimes mistrust, at the service of humanity.

• *It's true that your oral expression, through speeches or in some of the interviews or press conferences, has resulted in a lot of valuable*

2. *Carlos, the Dawn Is No Longer beyond Our Reach* is a long biographical prose poem written by Tomás Borge while in prison; begun when he received news of the death, in combat, of his old friend and comrade, cofounder and indisputable leader of the FSLN, Carlos Fonseca.

material. And it's logical, isn't it? Because of your historic role. But I know you write poetry, that you have written it and that you continue to write it. I remember, too, a children's story, a very beautiful story that was published a few months ago, in El Nuevo Amanecer Cultural [The New Dawn, *a cultural supplement of the independent newspaper,* The New Daily]. *And so you are a poet! Isn't it true that you write, in rare moments of spare time?*

Tomás: Well, I'm in the habit of being underground. Now that I'm not a guerrilla fighter anymore, now that I'm no longer clandestine in political terms, I think I have the right to remain underground in a literary sense. I'm a persecuted, underground poet.

• *Okay. So I won't ask you anymore about your clandestine activities! Tomás, you already mentioned some authors, especially from your childhood and youth, who affected you, whom you liked. Or that you like today. What about more modern authors? Your readings as an adult? I am especially interested in what you said one time about when you were in prison, that long solitary night . . . the readings and authors that accompanied you in one way or another. Could you speak about them?*

Tomás: Well, prison was a long and difficult holiday for me. And I read the writers it was possible to sneak into my cell. Josefina brought me what she had on hand, and many of those authors weren't allowed into my cell.

I've mentioned Cortázar's presence, among the inevitable— and in that case, wonderful—readings I had while in prison. Like anyone else interested in culture, I've read most of the well-known modern authors in Latin America . . . their names may be something of a cliché at this point.

I think that aside from the extraordinary affinity I have with Julio Cortázar, for reasons of personal friendship and because of the profound admiration I have for his work, and apart from the fact that contact with Cortázar ended up with me forgetting the writer to keep before me the memory of the man, apart from the personal friendships I've had with such courageous and original writers as Gabriel García Márquez and Eduardo Galeano, as well as Carlos Fuentes, and some correspondence with [Juan Carlos] Onetti, I believe that the most extraordinary writer I know of, from a formal point of view, in terms of his literary quality per se, is Jorge Luís Borges.

Recently I've been rereading and rediscovering Jorge Luís Borges. Because I believe that if you see him as a writer, somehow apart from his naïveté and from his political aberrations, Jorge Luís Borges constitutes, in my opinion, the most sadly brilliant writer in the Spanish language in modern times.

• *What you say brings up a question, or a doubt: How is it possible for a writer like Borges, or [Louis Ferdinand] Celine (who was a fascist writer, also with a great literary gift)—how is it possible for such a writer to create so much life in his work and still defend death politically? Sometime this is difficult to understand. How do you understand there being so much distance between a writer's ideology and his literary production?*

Tomás: It's a terrible contradiction. Because in the case of Borges, and perhaps also of Céline, their literature is above their political narrowness. That is, they are extraordinary from the point of view of creating the architecture of a literary work: great buildings, beautiful expressions of art, independent of the moral and political qualities of those able to create such things.

Borges, concretely, is such a brilliant writer that I think humanity will someday forgive him his sins.

• *Which works by Borges are you reading at the moment?*

Tomás: Well, I'm reading his complete works!

• *I remember a short story by Borges—I don't remember the title—in which the whole story takes place in the memory of a man who is waiting to be executed, to be shot. And the story begins as a tear begins to trickle down his cheek; when it gets to the bottom, his life ends.*

Tomás: Those of us who have been close to death, though, know that the time it takes for a tear to roll down one's cheek is not enough to recall one's entire life. It's true that at that moment your anxiety can synthesize some concrete or relevant aspect of your life, but life is too long a film to be measured in the trickle of a tear.

• *Maybe that's an example of an instance in which Borges didn't really know what he was writing about.*

Tomás: What was happening, perhaps, is that at that moment Borges was examining his own conscience, because if we are dealing with introspection and self-examination, Borges's life must be a permanent agony.

• *Tomás, speaking now about current Nicaraguan literature, and revolutionary literature–although perhaps it's too soon to speak of a literature of the revolution, this literature is only beginning–but we can speak of moments, and the whole course of Nicaraguan literature has been so very rich in its expression. Are there any writers or poets today in Nicaragua you particularly like? Who has impressed you, or been useful to you in some way?*

Tomás: There *is* a Nicaraguan revolutionary literature, and it starts with the very beginning of literature in Nicaragua. Because Rubén Darío was a revolutionary writer, and not only in terms of form but in many aspects concerning content as well. And the literature of the "vanguard"–the literary expression of, among others, José Coronel Urtecho, Joaquín Pasos, and I think you must also include Manolo Cuadra and Pablo Antonio Cuadra–this was, in general, a literature that can be placed within the context of the revolution. Even Pablo Antonio sold his white head of hair and his horn-rimmed glasses to the devil; But his poetry doesn't belong to him anymore. It's been expropriated by the people; it belongs to the people, to our national culture.

Nicaraguan revolutionary literature doesn't begin on July 19, 1979. Although perhaps it begins to acquire a new dimension on that date. You have to remember that the majority of our best writers, of the best writers this country has produced–among them Sergio Ramírez and Ernesto Cardenal–have dedicated themselves almost entirely to political activities, to government. And this has prevented them from realizing their full potential as writers, as poets. This is the reason why the pioneers–and especially Ernesto Cardenal, probably the most distinguished poet of the Nicaraguan Revolution (and its Minister of Culture)–have not been able to contribute to the new literature in a systematic and sustained manner.

But new writers *have* emerged in this country—some of them a bit surprising, like Omar Cabezas—who are producing literature that is very closely linked to the new reality being lived in Nicaragua today, and who have even provoked inevitable contradictions about the role of literature in the revolutionary process.

In any case, the revolution has not yet lost its creativity or its imagination. And I hope it never does. Because the day we have a factory making straitjackets to control the creative capacity of our artists, that day our revolution will begin to grow old.

• *Tomás, all the writers you mention are men. Are there any women writers or poets who have impressed you here?*

Tomás: Yes. Apart from the extraordinary poetry, coming from her special sensibility, that Rosario Murillo writes, Gioconda Belli has made an important contribution to the form and content of a very beautiful creative literature. Among the women poets in Nicaragua, I believe these two *compañeras*—and I have been very close to their literature; I have followed them both in their poetic expression—constitute the highest expression of Nicaraguan women's literature.

• *Anything else?*

Tomás: I think it's very important to emphasize the need for our artistic expression being free as a bird. It would be the worst kind of mistake if we began to invent steel handcuffs to pressure, repress, limit, or deform our rich literary creation. If any writer is marginalized because of alleged political deviations, I think our revolution must be flexible in this respect, because political flexibility is preferable to political terrorism against literary creation. My view is that within a certain basic context of identification with the revolutionary process revolutionary writers must be allowed to grow their own wings so they can fly to whatever heights they please.

And I speak of all artistic expression in this respect. We have a unique musical tradition here. And this originality cannot be emasculated for historical reasons. We have a potential for pictorial art, and this potential has to be kept intact. We have possibilities for theater. But theater has to be a creative work and not a boring, ready-made message to systematically respond to specific political situations. We cannot put all these human creative possibilities inside a narrow circle in the name of a temporal slogan. It would be like trapping them in the circles of hell.

• *This certainly has to do with the debate going on here now . . . the doubts that have arisen among some writers in regard to what the writer's or creative person's specific role in the revolutionary process should be. One's role as a writer, as a creative person, because one's role as a human being, if one is a revolutionary . . . that's clear. This discussion seems to repeat itself in every revolutionary process, and it's okay, because each people must deal with this problem from the point of view of its own history, its own culture.*

Tomás: The role of the writer in the revolution is, first of all, to write well. And, in the second place, to write for the people. And in the third place, to gather the rich wealth of popular struggle, of the heroism of the people, of the people's feelings and daily life, of the everyday love, the hands that link, the eyes that follow one another, the daily expectations arising among human beings. And to express all this in a form which is beautiful. That's the duty of the writer. To write in such a way that people feel like reading what has been written. What's the point of writing something with a supposedly revolutionary content if no one is going to read it? In this respect, form and content must be in a dialectical relationship that the writer, in my opinion, should have engraved in indelible letters on his brow, on his fingertips, in his heart.

Dullness, literary bad taste—that's counterrevolutionary. Beauty is revolutionary, as long as beauty doesn't become a cult of form for its own sake, and the goal is to express the highest content of the people and their revolution.

The following is a partial list of other books by Margaret Randall:

Carlota: Poems and Prose from Havana, Vancouver, B.C., Canada, New Star Publishers, 1978.

We (prose portraits), New York City, Smyrna Press, 1978.

Cuban Women Now, Toronto, Canadian Women's Educational Press, 1974. (With Spanish-language editions published in Mexico, Cuba, Venezuela and Colombia; and a Dutch edition published in Amsterdam, Holland.)

Spirit of the People: Vietnamese Women Two Years from the Geneva Accords, Vancouver, B.C., Canada, New Star Press, 1975. (Spanish-language edition published by Siglo XXI Editores, S.A., Mexico City, 1975).

Inside the Nicaraguan Revolution: The Story of Doris Tijerino, Vancouver, B.C., Canada, New Star Publishers, 1978. (The Spanish-language version of this book published by Extemporaneos, S.A., Mexico City, 1976; the Dutch edition published in Amsterdam, Holland, 1978).

Sandino's Daughters, Vancouver, B.C., Canada, 1981. (With a Spanish-language edition published by Siglo XXI, Mexico, in 1981; a Portuguese edition published by Editorial Global, Sao Paulo, Brazil, 1983; and an edition published in the Dominican Republic in 1983.)

Christians in the Nicaraguan Revolution, Vancouver, B.C., Canada, New Star Publishers, 1983. (With a Spanish-language edition published by Editorial Nueva Nicaragua, Managua, in 1984.

Cuban Women: Twenty Years Later (with photographs by Judy Janda), New York City, Smyrna Press, 1980.

Let's Go!, London, England, Cape-Goliard Publishers, 1970. (Selection of poems by the Guatemalan Otto-René Castillo. This book, long out of print, has been reissued by Curbstone Press, Willimantic, CT.)

Breaking The Silences, Poems by 25 Cuban Women Poets, Vancouver, B.C., Canada, Pulp Press, 1981.

Carlos, Dawn Is No Longer Beyond Our Reach, Vancouver, B.C., Canada, 1984. (A long prose poem by Tomás Borge.)